faithful

Herald Press
PO Box 866, Harrisonburg, Virginia 22803
www.HeraldPress.com

Library of Congress Cataloging-in-Publication Data
Names: Wiebe, Kevin, author.
Title: Faithful in small things : how to serve the needy when you're one of
   them / Kevin Wiebe.
Description: Harrisonburg, Virginia : Herald Press, 2021. | Includes
   bibliographical references.
Identifiers: LCCN 2020046183 (print) | LCCN 2020046184 (ebook) |
   ISBN 9781513807744 (paperback) | ISBN 9781513807751 (hardcover) |
   ISBN 9781513807768 (ebook)
Subjects: LCSH: Church work with the poor. | Poverty—Religious
   aspects—Christianity.
Classification: LCC BV639.P6 W54 2021 (print) | LCC BV639.P6 (ebook) |
   DDC 261.8/325—dc23
LC record available at https://lccn.loc.gov/2020046183
LC ebook record available at https://lccn.loc.gov/2020046184

Study guides are available for many Herald Press titles at www.HeraldPress.com.

FAITHFUL IN SMALL THINGS
© 2021 by Herald Press, Harrisonburg, Virginia 22803. 800-245-7894.
   All rights reserved.
Library of Congress Control Number: 2020046183
International Standard Book Number: 978-1-5138-0774-4 (paperback); 978-1-
5138-0775-1 (hardcover); 978-1-5138-0776-8 (ebook)
Printed in United States of America
Cover design by Merrill Miller

Unless otherwise noted, Scriptures are taken from the *Holy Bible, New International Version*®, NIV®. Copyright © 1973, 1978, 1984, 2011 by Biblica, Inc.™ Used
by permission of Zondervan. All rights reserved worldwide. www.zondervan.
com. The "NIV" and "New International Version" are trademarks registered in the
United States Patent and Trademark Office by Biblica, Inc.™

Scripture quotations marked (NLT) are taken from the *Holy Bible, New Living
Translation*, copyright © 1996, 2004, 2015 by Tyndale House Foundation. Used
by permission of Tyndale House Publishers, Inc., Carol Stream, Illinois 60188. All
rights reserved.

25 24 23 22 21   10 9 8 7 6 5 4 3 2 1

faithful in small things

HOW TO SERVE THE NEEDY
WHEN YOU'RE
ONE OF THEM

Kevin Wiebe

HERALD
PRESS

Harrisonburg, Virginia

Joe & Mary

*Thank you for your example to me of loving people
in countless and ordinary ways.*

Contents

Foreword

THIS IS AN EXCELLENT BOOK precisely because it is so unusual.

It is unusual in many ways—but especially because it combines things that so often are not held together. This book is full of both solid biblical theology and practical, concrete suggestions. Author Kevin Wiebe is equally adept at citing the relevant literature and telling powerful personal stories. He is equally passionate about the heart of historic orthodox theology and working for peace and justice in society. The book helps the reader understand that when we seek to empower poor people, we sometimes succeed in big ways and sometimes fail miserably—and often just in tiny ways that are still significant.

This book flows from the heart of a person who has lived what he preaches. Wiebe has personally experienced grinding poverty and severe illness. He candidly shares his failures as well as his successes. Much of the wisdom of the book flows precisely from the fact that the author pastors not an urban megachurch, but a small, rural congregation.

This book is full of practical wisdom and gripping stories. Reading it helps one understand how to take small, concrete steps to love and empower hurting neighbors. Sometimes even a smile can lead to the transformation of a broken person. And if the smile only warms the heart of a child or a person who is homeless for a moment, it is still significant and well worth giving.

Wiebe really wants us to end poverty in our world. But he wants us to do that in the name of, and in the power of, the risen Lord Jesus. And he wants us to know that even when our best efforts produce only modest results, or even fail, we need not be discouraged. Small things are important. And we can learn from our worst failures.

Careful reading of *Faithful in Small Things* will bring large benefits.

Ronald J. Sider
Emeritus professor of theology, holistic ministry,
and public policy at Palmer Theological
Seminary of Eastern University

Introduction

WHEN I WAS GROWING UP, my parents shared our home with many different people. Our door was open to an often-revolving group of houseguests, most of them people my parents met who had no place else to go. Some stayed a few days, others a few weeks or months, and others for years. Every person's situation was different, but they were all welcome to share whatever we had. We always lived in small towns, which meant that we didn't see people living on the streets quite as often as one might in larger cities. Nearby urban areas had shelters, soup kitchens, and other resources that made it easier to survive, so those without a home would usually find their way there. I sometimes wondered how my parents came to know so many people in need in our small town, because just by looking at our housemates it might have been hard to tell that they didn't have homes. They didn't push shopping carts around town or sleep on public sidewalks in the middle of town. Their clothes weren't fancy, but neither were ours, so I thought they were just normal people. They *were* just normal people, and many became life-long friends. For the vast majority, their need for shelter arose from no fault of their own. Even so, they found themselves in the extraordinary situation of not knowing where they would sleep until they got their lives back on track.

Despite the way we helped others, we were not immune to poverty either, and just before my ninth birthday, we lost our home, my dad lost his business, and we were forced to move about eight hundred kilometers away, relying on my widowed grandmother until we recovered financially. I consider myself privileged in many ways, not just because my family had a roof over our heads to share with others—though we too lost that roof at one point and needed others to help us—but because I have so many friends with whom I have shared my journey of life. While we were often financially needy, I am privileged to have a wealth of stories, experiences, and relationships that have profoundly shaped who I am now. I learned from the lives of others who generously shared their stories with me, some by telling me about their journey, and others by walking with me for a while on a shared path. I believe that stories are powerful, and each one shared is like a precious jewel.

I have also learned a great deal from the people in the congregation where I serve as pastor. Most of our people moved to Canada from Mexico, and stories abound of desperate poverty—which was often the reason for their move. I have been privileged to get to know the amazing people in our rural congregation and to watch them live generously even amid their own financial hardships. Their stories motivate me and are also part of my inspiration for writing.

I am writing this book to ordinary people who may not be able to afford to take trips overseas but who read the words of the Bible and feel compelled by God to do something to make this world a better place. I am writing to those who may be living under the poverty line but who are still striving to make a difference in the world. Our culture often assumes that those with extensive financial means will be the ones to make the biggest difference in our world, but I strongly believe that ordinary people have the most holistic and long-lasting impact. I believe that God has a unique and powerful role for all of us to help others who struggle with poverty. Resist the urge to downplay your own importance in these matters simply because of the small number in your bank account—there is a good chance that you are positioned to do an immense amount of good, not despite your financial struggles but precisely because of them. Firsthand experiences with poverty provide us an education more comprehensive than a university degree, not to mention the fact that those with less are many, and this strength in numbers also makes us mighty.

My hope is that over the course of reading this book, you will take stock of your own life and offer what you can to help those around you. I want to challenge some unhealthy ideas that sometimes lurk in our churches, and I hope to inspire us all to live more compassionate and generous lives.

In a relatively small book such as this, there are certain complexities and nuances that will not be adequately covered, and as such I expect that this book might cause some rigorous debate. We all have wisdom to bring to the table, and I'm sure that I could learn much from every person reading this. Regardless of whether we are politically conservative or liberal, whether we are Mennonites, Pentecostals, or from the Salvation Army, if we are Christians then we have the common ground of being followers of Jesus and believing that we have a part to play in God's work in the world. My goal is to add something to this conversation and bring this topic to the forefront of our minds, with the hopes that we can each resolve to live out our faith in all kinds of ordinary and profound ways to serve the world around us and so bring glory to God.

This book is divided into four sections. The first one is focused on biblical foundations that have shaped the way I think and teach on this topic. The second section is about challenging the way we think about poverty, and the importance of relationships and healthy attitudes in how we seek to address poverty. In the third section, we will discuss more hands-on principles that can be used in how we live and work in the world as we try to make a difference. The last section is about what can happen when we take the brave step of serving others, including some ways we can fail, and what to do when that happens.

While you will find a great deal of food for thought in the coming pages, my aim is to help expand and further this very important conversation, not to be the final word on the subject. The journey we are embarking on in this book is an important one, and I am honored that you have chosen to travel it together with me as your conversation guide.

PART 1: **The Bible on Poverty**

The Bible has a lot to say about money and poverty, justice, generosity, and selflessness. There are also many lessons in Scripture about the dangers of greed, oppression, and inequality. These messages in God's Word help guide, motivate, and shape our actions and our character in relationship to money and poverty. In the words of community development specialists and professors Steve Corbett and Brian Fikkert, "Although the Bible is not a textbook on poverty alleviation, it does give us valuable insights into the nature of human beings, of history, of culture, and of God to point us in the right direction."[1] This first section focuses on some of the very important lessons the Bible offers as we seek to serve our world.

ONE

The Poverty in Us All

"WE'RE MOVING TO LA CRETE." The words hung in the air like my dad's cigarette smoke as my eight-year-old mind grappled with all the implications of that statement. We lived close to Edmonton, Alberta, but my parents were from a small town in the far northern reaches of the province, close to the Northwest Territories, to which we were now returning. The bank was foreclosing on our home and my dad's business was in a tough spot, so we were moving up north to live in my grandmother's basement.

I'd always known that money was tight. I had memories of watching my mother dig through the couch for nickels and dimes so we could buy milk for my baby sister. Yet we always had food to eat, and other people often came to our home for a meal or a place to sleep. But after housing so many people, it was now our turn to ask for help and to sleep on the floor in someone else's home. I was about to lose not just my physical home but my friends, church, and community as well. How could this be happening?

My questions about my own family's experience of homelessness led, in later years, to questions about why poverty exists in this world and how to define it. Were we poor because we had very little? Or because we lost our home? Or were we rich because we were able to help others in a small way? How we define poverty is important if we truly wish to help reduce it. Fortunately, the first pages of the Bible offer some clues.

The Genesis story depicts four kinds of human relationships, and reveals how the root of all poverty can be traced back to the breakdown of those relationships. The Bible's origin story informs us that when God made humanity, we were made in the very image of our Creator. So who is this God, in whose image we are fashioned? Bryant L. Myers is a professor, author, and development expert who used this very important question as the basis for a model about the causes of poverty.[1] God is a relational being: Father, Son, and Holy Spirit. We too are relational beings, and it is the breakdown of our relationships that result in various kinds of poverty.

Myers outlines the four kinds of human relationships depicted in the Genesis story: the relationship we have with God, others, ourselves, and creation. In the story of Adam and Eve in Genesis 3, we see that their sin drove a wedge into their relationship with God; they hid from their Creator. Adam blamed Eve, who blamed someone else still—which is evidence of their broken relationship with each other. They now felt shame about their bodies and guilt for their actions, revealing pain in the way they viewed themselves. Something was also broken in their relationship with the earth, which required that Adam and Eve toil to grow food and scratch out their livelihood. When any one of these relationships falls apart, the result is some form of poverty. Myers's four-part framework has helped me make sense of a lot of what I've experienced of poverty in the world. While poverty does include a lack of money at our disposal, it is so much more than that. Let's take a deeper look at each of these four aspects of poverty.

US AND GOD

When sin entered the world, Adam and Eve were cut off from their immediate access to God. Pastors and theologians talk about the history of the world as having several important events: *creation, fall,* and *redemption.* Some add *consummation* as a fourth category, referring to our hope for eternity when there will be no more poverty of any sort. The first two of these categories, creation and fall, take up only a few short chapters at the beginning of Genesis. God created the world, and we rebelled, allowing sin to enter the world. The redemption part comes about ultimately in Jesus, who came to earth to restore the relationship between us and God. From the perspective of the Bible, the relationship between God and people is of utmost importance. That relationship is one of the main points of the whole book—the origin of how our relationship with God broke down, warnings about what drives us even further from God, and stories about what is needed to restore that relationship.

What does our relationship with God have to do with poverty? First, it points us to the reality of a type of spiritual poverty, in which our spiritual selves are starving because we are not connected to the source of true spiritual strength. In John 15, Jesus describes our connection to God as that of a branch on a vine: without being connected to the vine, a branch will wither and die. In John 4, he describes what God offers as "living water." There is something about being connected to God that nourishes us, strengthens us, and gives us life. It is our relationship with God that helps transform us into people who care more about the people God cares about and do the things that God wants us to do. Our relationship with God can be described as twofold. Getting right with God is good for us; it helps strengthen us, helps us face whatever life throws our way, and shows us that God loves us without condition. Second, being right with God begins to change the way we see the world around us. Our heart begins to break for the plight of those around us, and we begin to desire seeing God's will be done "on earth as it is in heaven" (Matthew 6:10).

Throughout the pages of Scripture, there are accounts of those who stray from God, who pervert justice and embrace selfishness, who exploit others and create systems that keep people in poverty. The rich get richer, the poor get poorer, and God grows furious with humanity for doing this. Check out Isaiah 1, or Amos 5, and you will read about how deeply our relationships with others are connected to our relationship with God. Even a cursory reading of the Bible reveals many lessons about how to live in this world, lessons about not stealing from or oppressing others. Lessons about integrity and standing against corruption. All of this is part of following God's plan for humanity.

US AND OTHERS

Poverty can be caused by broken relationships between ourselves and others. Think about a woman and her children who flee an abusive husband and father in search of safety. In many cases, the husband may be the primary breadwinner, forcing the woman to become for the first time the sole financial provider for her family. This while also having to seek security and spend time, energy, and money dealing with the effects of emotional trauma in her children, all the while trying to find healing for herself. The breakdown of marriage relationships often results in material poverty for women and children (and sometimes for men too), even while the broken relationship itself is a form of relational poverty.

We have all been hurt by others, and I suspect that we have all done something to hurt another person as well. The consequences of these painful choices can result in poverty. Consider a young person experiencing chronic bullying. These actions can cause depression, anxiety, or other mental illness, and it doesn't take a college degree to know that mental illness is a significant cause of poverty in a financial sense.

The example of bullying helps us see another aspect of relational breakdown: the danger of victim blaming. When we talk about a breakdown in relationships, most of us will immediately think of two people whose actions are both equally, or nearly equally, responsible for the damage done to the relationship. The reality, however, is that there are countless scenarios in which a broken relationship between two people is the result of one person's actions, such as in the case of the average schoolyard bully. As adults, we should have compassion on the young bully too, but this doesn't mean that those harmed by the bully are at fault for the bully's torment.

While there are many cases where both parties have made mistakes, it takes only one person to cause a broken relationship. When it comes to our relationships with others, we should also consider the relationship between an individual and the groups around that person, such as governments or other cultural groups. These relationships between ourselves and other groups can also be damaged and broken. This kind of breakdown in relationship is what we could call systemic injustice, because it often involves the systems we use as humans to organize ourselves. Just as in relationships between two individuals, a breakdown can be caused by both parties or just one, and it is important to figure out the underlying causes in order to properly address them.

Broken relationships are not the only cause of poverty; an absence of healthy relationships is itself a form of poverty. Mother Teresa famously talked about the devastation of loneliness. She said, "There are many in the world who are dying for a piece of bread but there are many more dying for a little love. . . . There's a hunger for love, as there is a hunger for God."[2] She did not think that the most terrible poverty was leprosy or a lack of worldly goods, but rather a lack of healthy relationships with others.

US AND OURSELVES

At times we can be our own worst enemies. The beliefs we have about ourselves can cause or even entrench many kinds of poverty in our lives, be it financial, emotional, spiritual, or mental.

In *Reckless Faith: Let Go and Be Led*, author Beth Guckenberger tells a story that illustrates an impact of poverty on our relationship with ourselves that is devastatingly common. Guckenberger was working with orphaned children in Mexico, where she met a child named Isaac who was a very talented artist but struggled all through high school. Isaac struggled to finish high school for the same reasons many orphaned children do—Isaac was bullied, and felt that he didn't belong at school and did not feel worthy enough to attend. His false sense of inadequacy ran so deep that he almost quit many times. Guckenberger writes that every day Isaac was "walking into a school situation in which, over and over again, he had to prove that he deserved to be there."[3] Eventually, he was given the opportunity to go to college, and while he did end up going, his profound sense of unworthiness almost sabotaged this opportunity before it even began.

For those who didn't grow up in poverty, this struggle can be hard to understand. Society divides itself across all kinds of lines, including how much money you have. I took note of Isaac's story when I first read it because it resonated so much with me. Compared to Isaac's upbringing I would be considered wealthy. I had two parents and I never went hungry. Yet something goes on in our own minds that is a common phenomenon around the world, despite cultural differences and varying concepts of what constitutes poverty. While we will talk about this more later in the book, when we internalize our physical poverty, it changes our view of ourselves. Instead of boldly taking an opportunity given to us, we question whether we are worthy to accept such an opportunity. If we determine that we are unworthy of such opportunities or don't belong in the ivory towers or the halls of power, we may reject those opportunities, just as Isaac very nearly rejected his opportunity to go to college. This was one of the reasons I also nearly didn't go to university, and the reason why I felt like dropping out many times. My wife deserves a lot of credit for helping me achieve my goals instead of giving up before I've given it my best. As I've offered advice to others who have the opportunity to advance their education, I've found that it is remarkably common for people with less financial means to doubt their worthiness to do something as simple as furthering their education.

This type of broken relationship with ourselves causes dreadful poverty of all kinds, whether through sabotaging ourselves by not taking opportunities given to us, or by driving others away with self-destructive behavior. The relationship we have with ourselves has drastic consequences when it comes to the root causes of poverty.

US AND CREATION

The last of these relationships is between us and creation, or our physical environment and other creatures. This is blatantly evident in even a cursory look at ecology; there are some very down-to-earth ways in which our relationship to the land we live on causes poverty.

My wife spent some time living and working in a community in northwestern Ontario called Grassy Narrows. Over the years, CBC News has done some great work documenting the effects that mercury poisoning has had on the people of this remote community.[4] Years ago, unrestrained industrial processes poisoned the English-Wabigoon River, and the effects have been felt for decades and continue to this day. The community's main water supply was poisoned, along with the fish, which are traditionally one of the community's main sources of food. As you might imagine, the people who live there suffer much higher than average medical problems, directly caused by or complicated by mercury poisoning. There are many neurological problems, such as numbness in extremities, seizures, and cognitive delays[5]—not to mention all the psychological trauma of watching loved ones go through such difficulties. A broken or unhealthy relationship with our environment where our world is abused and poisoned causes poverty among the people who live on that land.

The community of La Crete, where my family moved after losing our home, is an old-fashioned rural farming community, and many of the local Christian farmers practiced some of the Old Testament laws about leaving the land to rest every seven years. In the age we live in now, this is a rare thing, since farmers can simply add fertilizer to the land to make it yield crops. It was interesting to listen to the farmers talk at coffee shops: those who allowed their land to rest periodically did not need nearly as much fertilizer, if any, to get their crops to grow. Those who did not let the land rest needed increasing amounts of fertilizer, because the land was overworked, and the soil was more or less dead without the addition of those nutrients. Imagine the world in the not-so-distant past, before the technology we have today: overworking your land for short-term gain meant destroying the crop yields of the future. Farmers had to live in a proper relationship with the ground they worked in order to avoid poverty.

Think of the biblical example from Genesis 13, where Abraham and Lot could no longer live so closely together. They had both grown wealthy with plenty of cattle and livestock. The text tells us that "the land could not support them while they stayed together" (v. 6). In this story, they needed to spread out. If they tried to overuse the land, not only would that have negative effects on them physically, but it was already leading to a breakdown in relationships between the two households. They needed to respect the limits of the land in order to maintain health among their livestock and health in their relationships with one another. The same happened with the brothers Jacob and Esau in Genesis 36, where they had to move away from each other because "the land where they were staying could not support them both because of their livestock" (v. 7).

There are many examples throughout history where living in a broken relationship with our physical world results in various forms of poverty. Sometimes those relationships are broken intentionally for selfish gain, other times they are broken in ignorance by people not fully aware of the consequences of their actions—but either way, that kind of broken relationship is responsible for a lot of poverty in our world.

* * *

Instead of defining poverty as simply a lack of worldly goods, Bryant Myers defines it as a series of broken relationships that have consequences for us in every area of life. Steve Corbett and Brian Fikkert, in their very helpful book *When Helping Hurts*, also embrace Myers's framework. They demonstrate how this perspective not only lays a good foundation for understanding poverty, but also prevents a lot of mishaps along the way. Think of it this way: if doctors treat only your medical symptoms and fail to discover the root cause of your illness, they will often give you treatments that will not help and may even make things worse. A proper understanding of what causes an illness is needed in order to properly treat it. The same is true of poverty: properly understanding the cause of poverty can help with being more effective at reducing it and avoiding the harm we sometimes inflict.

When we define poverty more holistically, it helps us be more effective in helping others. Yet it also opens another door that many of us might be uncomfortable with: it invites us to uncover the ways in which we are still living in poverty.

Katie Taylor from Mennonite Central Committee in Ontario tells a story of when she was younger and helping at an urban ministry that provided meals for people living on the streets. She came to help others with great zeal and (mostly) good motives, wanting to help fix the problems that resulted in homelessness. As she was serving, she encountered a man from the street and began a conversation with him. Over the course of their conversation, she was humbled as she began to realize that this man had a faith in God much more profound than the one she had experienced up until then, and that her efforts to "fix" him were truly misguided. Did he have deep struggles? Absolutely. Yet his struggles were much more complicated than she was able to fix, and his faith in God even while living in tremendous poverty was something to learn from and be inspired by. Katie discovered that as she was trying to reduce someone else's poverty, she came face-to-face with spiritual poverty in her own life that resulted from a naive understanding of suffering and a view of poverty based superficially on material wealth.

Many of us in the Global North experience a (financial) standard of living much higher than that of the rest of the world. We generally know this, and many of us want to leave this world in better shape than we have found it. We want to help and we want to share. The fact that you are reading this book reveals several things: First, that you can read. There are many for whom literacy is only a distant dream, even within my congregation. Second, you have spare time enough to read a book such as this, and don't have to spend all your time working multiple jobs to make a living. Third, unless you are borrowing this book or it was a gift, you have enough disposable income to purchase it. And fourth, you likely wouldn't pick up a book like this unless you actually wanted to make a difference in this world, and so it is likely that you have fairly good motives coming into this.

While having a proper understanding of the root causes of poverty can help us do better at serving others, it also has another purpose that is just as profound. It uncovers the poverty that exists within ourselves. The assumptions that might be made about the average person reading this are just that—assumptions. And if they are at all accurate, and you find yourself among those of this world that have more money and stuff than others around them, then you might be tempted to gloss over the poverty that does exist in your own life.

While I believe it is important to be thankful for what we have, and to not delve into a world of endless complaining, I also believe it is vitally important that we all realize our own poverty, for our own sakes, but also for the sake of others.

When doing poverty reduction work, it can be incredibly easy to fall into a mindset of *us* and *them*. We think that *they* are in poverty, and *we* can help them. While *we* may be the ones with more financial resources, it is a mistake to put ourselves on a pedestal and to label *them* as if they are somehow more defective than we are. If we truly understand our own poverty, then we will know how little we truly have to offer. This doesn't mean we shouldn't offer it, but rather it changes *how* we offer it. Instead of offering it out of a god complex, we offer it in humility. Instead of seeing others as a project, we can begin to see them as fellow bearers of God's image who have simply experienced broken relationships in a different way than we have.

In the story of the Tower of Babel, the people came together to make a name for themselves and built a large tower. It was something these people were proud of, and it was a major accomplishment in their day. It would have taken a lot of resources, and the writer of Genesis says, "The LORD came down to see the city and the tower" (Genesis 11:5). To the Hebrew reader, this is akin to a parent stooping down to see the little sandcastle their toddler is building. From God's perspective, no matter how much money we have or how great we think we are, God looks at our supposed success the way a parent looks at that sandcastle; sure, it might be fun and interesting, but it will soon get swept away by the waves. The reality is that we have profound needs and forms of poverty deep within our being.

As we approach others whom we label as "people in poverty," we should also examine the forms of poverty in ourselves. Before we come to believe that we have all the answers or that we are somehow better than the people we are serving, we would do well to remember that those who live in one form of poverty may in fact have much to teach us about the poverty we experience. Like Katie, whose financial state was better than that of a man who was homeless, but whose faith had much to be desired in comparison to his. After all, it was a murdered and homeless Middle Eastern man who brought the world eternal salvation.

TWO

The Murdered Homeless Man

I WAS IN EDMONTON, ALBERTA, at a music festival when I bumped into an acquaintance, a local musician named Joe whom my cohosts and I had interviewed on our radio show. It was a beautiful autumn night, the concerts were over, and we stood at the edge of the outdoor amphitheater under a beautiful starlit sky. After Joe and I talked for a while about music, our conversation turned to faith. I don't remember the context of how or why I spoke the name of Jesus, but I will never forget Joe's response. At the mention of the name of Jesus, Joe smiled, sat down, and motioned for me to join him. After a few moments of silence, he realized I was watching him as he sat in what appeared to be a state of peaceful bliss. He politely apologized and then said, "I just love Jesus so much, you know? And hearing you talk about him just made me so happy." To this day I have never witnessed someone who responded quite like Joe did that night.

Jesus is the central figure of Christianity. He is the Christ, a title that means the Messiah, the Son of God, the Anointed

One. The person of Jesus, known as "God in the flesh," stunningly describes himself as homeless and was murdered in one of the most painful ways possible. While his homelessness may differ from that of many people (he wandered because of his God-given mission to minister to humanity), he says that he had no place to lay his head (Luke 9:58). After his upbringing in poverty, Jesus ministered to others while not having a home to go to each night, and then was the victim of torture and homicide. While it was a state-sanctioned execution, it was murder all the same; the particulars of the story indicate that crowds of people chanted for the government to crucify him, despite a finding of innocence. Between the conniving religious leaders, the threatening crowds, the state, and the soldiers who carried out the execution, Jesus' death was not just or fair. This is all very significant because it shows us that Jesus lived in solidarity with those on the margins and those who experienced poverty and injustice. His life was not one of taking things for himself but one of giving to humanity, even to the point of giving his own life.

At some point in the early church, those who were disciples of Jesus became known as Christians. We read about this in the book of Acts, and the name simply means one who is a follower of the Christ. It is no small matter that the life and teachings of Jesus demonstrate God's love and care for those on the margins. While we may avert our gaze when we see poverty, Jesus didn't avoid those who were suffering under its burden. In fact, it is through Jesus that we come to see even more clearly the character of the God of the Bible. As a teenager I thought that God must have had a personality change somewhere between the Old Testament and the New Testament, but as I grew in my faith I came to see, through Jesus, the remarkably consistent character of God and the ongoing love God shows humanity. As Christian activist and author Shane Claiborne has said, "The God that lives in Jesus isn't different from the God of the Old Testament."[1]

Before taking a look at the life of Jesus, let's take a step back for a moment to wrestle with some important theology. Why do so many Christians today focus so much on Jesus? Christianity, after all, teaches the Trinity. In the words of the Athanasian Creed, "We worship one God in Trinity, and Trinity in Unity; neither confounding the Persons, nor dividing the Essence. For there is one Person of the Father; another of the Son; and another of the Holy Ghost. But the Godhead of the Father, of the Son, and of the Holy Ghost, is all one; the Glory equal, the Majesty coeternal." So why not focus on God the Father, or on the Holy Spirit? The reality is that if we ignore God the Father or the Holy Spirit, we will not fully understand Jesus either.

Pastor Albert Loewen argues that Jesus didn't primarily care about helping the poor. The first time I heard this, I was shocked and wondered if we were reading the same Bible. He went on to explain that Jesus was primarily concerned with following the will of God the Father. Why is this important? Why does it matter that Jesus was primarily concerned with doing the will of the Father, above all else? What does trinitarian theology have to do with discussions of poverty? Musician and activist Steve Bell puts it nicely: "Especially those of us who grew up in evangelical culture, we make Jesus the endgame of our faith, and Jesus is not the endgame, it's the life of the Trinity. Jesus comes to pave a way and to invite us into that delight and that mutuality. What we have with the Trinity is each member completely pouring out themselves for the sake of the others—mutual flourishing. It's an emptying, becoming impoverished for the sake of the other, and that is really profound."[2]

If we are going to consider what we as Christians should do in helping others, it is wise to start with what God has done. Professor of theology Joseph Mangina writes, "For ethics to be Christian, the theologian must think first of all in terms of what God has done, and only then proceed to consider what that implies about human beings and their choices."[3] Before we look to the work of God in history, let us first consider the relationships among the members of the Trinity.

When Jesus was in the garden of Gethsemane, before his arrest and subsequent torture and crucifixion, he spent time in prayer. In prayer he asks God, if it is possible, to remove the suffering that is about to take place—but then he says something else. He prays, "Yet not my will, but yours be done" (Luke 22:42). Jesus sought to be obedient to the will of the Father. Furthermore, we read in the Epistles that Jesus, "who, being in very nature God, did not consider equality with God something to be used to his own advantage; rather, he made himself nothing by taking the very nature of a servant, being made in human likeness. And being found in appearance as a man, he humbled himself by becoming obedient to death—even death on a cross!" (Philippians 2:6-8). Jesus, who is God, left the riches of heaven and came to earth in the form of a man in order to serve God the Father, being obedient even to the point of death. Yet this last passage also tells us of God the Father's response to the work of Jesus: "Therefore God exalted him to the highest place and gave him the name that is above every name" (v. 9). We see Jesus pouring himself out for the sake of God the Father, and then we see Jesus being lifted up above all others, to the place of highest honor.

While the role of the Holy Spirit in the Trinity is not quite as clearly spoken of in the Bible, we do see that whenever the Holy Spirit is mentioned as being active in a given story, it is assumed that God is at work, and the Holy Spirit acts in accordance with the will of God, just as Jesus does.

In fact, this kind of mystery surrounding the Holy Spirit helps us understand why so many of us have come to focus on Jesus. While the Holy Spirit is just as fully God as the person of Jesus, the Spirit is a bit harder to think about. In Jesus, however, we have a picture of God in human form. We read that Jesus is "the image of the invisible God" (Colossians 1:15). Jesus teaches his disciples that "anyone who has seen me has seen the Father" (John 14:9). Later on, when Jesus returns to heaven, he promises that the Holy Spirit is going to be given to them after he leaves (Acts 1:5). But then in the great commission, before his ascension, he tells the disciples, "Surely I am with you always, to the very end of the age" (Matthew 28:20). Here again, just as Jesus blurs the lines between knowing him and knowing God the Father, so too he blurs the lines between his presence as God in the flesh in the person of Jesus and God's presence with us through the Holy Spirit. As Claiborne says, "We can see in Jesus what God is really like in a concrete way. . . . Sometimes it's hard for me to wrap my arms around the God who is the 'I AM WHO I AM'—God really brings things down to earth in Jesus."[4]

This is why so many of us focus on Jesus: the person of Jesus gives us a clearer picture of who God is, and an example for us to follow. For this reason, Anabaptists have historically viewed Jesus as central to our faith, and central to how we read and understand the rest of the Bible.[5] It is not that in focusing on Jesus we exclude God the Father and the Holy Spirit; rather, it is through Jesus that we can come to better understand the Trinity.

As we consider the way that the members of the Trinity love and serve one another, we see a powerful example for the church. This application, however, isn't just speculative or reading something into the Scriptures. The author of Philippians writes, "In your relationships with one another, have the same mindset as Christ Jesus" (Philippians 2:5), and then goes on to explain how Jesus humbled himself to become a servant of others. Such an example is both profound and powerful, as our approach to poverty is often mired in pride and steeped in judgment against those we claim to be serving.

If we are to first consider the work of God in helping us determine how we treat others, then the obvious question is, How did God treat people in poverty throughout history? We can see throughout the Hebrew Scriptures an incredible care for those who were oppressed or impoverished. We see instructions like "Do not oppress a foreigner; you yourselves know how it feels to be foreigners, because you were foreigners in Egypt" (Exodus 23:9). This kind of instruction regarding foreigners is repeated many times throughout the Bible. There are instructions about leaving some of the harvest in the field so that those struggling with poverty can glean from it (Leviticus 19:9-10). The book of Proverbs is also littered with instructions to care for others, such as "Whoever oppresses the poor shows contempt for their Maker, but whoever is kind to the needy honors God" (Proverbs 14:31).

Then there are passages like Isaiah 1 and Amos 5 that reveal a God who *hates* and *detests* the religious activities of Israel. Why? After all, many of their rituals are prescribed in the law. God didn't hate their worship, but rather hated that their rituals were a mask for what was really going on—or worse yet, that their worship enabled oppression and injustice. God despised the way they turned the privilege of being the people of God into a religion that oppressed others and rewarded corruption, instead of being a people through whom God could bless the whole world (Genesis 12:1-3). God desired to see "justice roll on like a river, righteousness like a never-failing stream!" (Amos 5:24).

The Hebrew Scriptures are full of stories that demonstrate God's care for people and God's compassion for the oppressed, the marginalized, and those living in poverty. Then comes the incarnation, where God "became flesh and made his dwelling among us" (John 1:14). This, of course, is Jesus. When we think of Jesus, "the pioneer and perfecter of faith" (Hebrews 12:2), what do we see in his example? The very act of the incarnation demonstrates a kind of solidarity with humanity. Jesus left the riches of heaven to come to earth as a human being, not growing up in the halls of power and luxury, but being born in a barn and fleeing to Egypt as a child refugee. While Joseph was a carpenter and would have been able to provide for the most basic necessities, we also see that when Mary and Joseph offer a sacrifice, they offer birds, the prescribed offering for those who were not wealthy enough to afford a lamb.

When a man wanted to follow Jesus, Jesus gave him the most peculiar reply. He tells the man, "Foxes have dens and birds have nests, but the Son of Man has no place to lay his head" (Luke 9:58). While many of us might be tempted to think that Jesus could use a lesson on marketing, he reveals something to us about the God who came to earth in the flesh: he describes himself as homeless. The God who made the world makes his way through it as someone without a stable place to lay his head. While I am not going to suggest that Christians should all become homeless—though there are worse suggestions out there—I will suggest that Jesus' life as someone who did not have a place to lay his head ought to shape the way we view those in our own communities who suffer from homelessness. The fact that Jesus, as a child, was a refugee who fled for his life, should shape our response to refugees in our world today. And since Jesus "came to seek and to save the lost" (Luke 19:10), that should affect the way we view those who have lost their way.

There have been moments in ministry when I have heard people use the words of Jesus to communicate that we need not care about those in poverty by saying something like "Since Jesus said, 'The poor you will always have with you,' then we don't need to try to help." That's a quote from Matthew 26, where a woman anoints Jesus' feet with perfume that was exorbitantly expensive. Those present criticize the woman, saying that they could have made better use of it by selling it and giving the proceeds to the poor. It sounds noble enough, at least at first. But Jesus rebukes them by saying, "The poor you will always have with you, but you will not always have me. When she poured this perfume on my body, she did it to prepare me for burial. Truly I tell you, wherever this gospel is preached throughout the world, what she has done will also be told, in memory of her" (Matthew 26:11-13). This perfume was an extravagant gift, but it was appropriate given what was about to happen to Jesus. The part that people sometimes focus on, however, is actually a reference to the book of Deuteronomy, which says, "There will always be poor people in the land. Therefore I command you to be openhanded toward your fellow Israelites who are poor and needy in your land" (Deuteronomy 15:11). The logic of the passage Jesus is quoting is exactly the opposite of the way some people use it today. The contextual understanding of Jesus' use of the phrase "The poor you will always have with you" isn't that we don't need to care about helping those in poverty, but rather that because they are always here, we need to be continually serving others generously—although in this instance an extravagant gift given to Jesus was beautiful and perfectly acceptable. In other words, there should never be a time when the people of God fail, because of willful inaction, to care for those who experience poverty.

Throughout the ministry of Jesus, we see him spending time with those whom the rest of the world had cast aside. Repeatedly in the Gospels we find Jesus healing the sick, feeding the hungry, touching the lepers, and eating with those who were social outcasts. Jesus didn't play by the rules of the world, and instead preferred to follow the will of God. Claiborne says, "One of the most radical things [Jesus] did was have subversive friendship, you know, build relationship with the wrong people and have dinner with people you just weren't supposed to have dinner with. In the end, I think that when things will really change is when we see that the gospel is lived out at dinner tables and in living rooms, and our friendships need to begin to change."[6]

The Salvation Army is remarkably good at living this out. Out of their love of God and devotion to following Jesus, they engage in ministries that demonstrate the love of God in ways that are understandable, helping people in need. William and Catherine Booth were the founders of the Salvation Army, and William Booth is quoted as saying, "There have been men with greater brains than I, even with greater opportunities, but from the day I got the poor of London on my heart and caught a vision of what Jesus Christ could do with me and them, on that day I made up my mind that God should have all of William Booth there was."[7] This was the mission to which he dedicated his life. When the Booths began their ministry, this wasn't something new; this is an ancient way to live, something God longs to see us doing. Yet it is something far too many have left undone, both historically and today. The Booths are now historic role models because they simply lived this out, and inspired so many others to join them on this ancient path.

In the New Testament, one way the writers speak about the church is as the body of Christ. In such an analogy, Jesus is the head over the body, and the members of the church make up the other parts of the body. This means that if we want to know how Jesus would want us to treat someone today, we must consider how he treated people in the Gospels. For Jesus to be the head of the body means that the body works at doing that which Jesus desires the body to do.

At times when I look at the church, I shudder to think of the images we see of Christ's body in the world. Instead of serving with love, we bite and devour one another. Instead of bandaging wounds, we attempt an amputation. While these terrible stories exist and we must own them as a church, thankfully there are also times when the church does in fact serve as the very hands and feet of Jesus.

It is Jesus who is the savior of the world, and it is through Jesus that salvation came to the world. Though he was murdered on a Roman cross, that did not mark his defeat. When he rose from the grave, his resurrection marked a victory over the forces of darkness, and brought hope and salvation to all who would call on his name. This murdered "homeless" man changed the world. When Jesus ascended into heaven, he left the entire ministry of the church in the hands of eleven disciples and the Holy Spirit. And that was enough. They didn't have a massive bank account or stockpiles of gold. They didn't have elaborate education beyond their time walking with Jesus. From an organizational standpoint, Jesus left the church in a precarious position at best. Yet this is in line with his entire ministry—Jesus established what Anabaptist scholar Donald Kraybill calls an "upside-down kingdom."[8] It is a great irony that when we talk about poverty, so many of us think about our own lack of money and then curtail our own efforts to serve before we've even begun. Sometimes we believe that because we, too, struggle with paying the bills, we cannot make a difference, even though the example of Jesus shows that money isn't the greatest currency and that even death doesn't have the final say.

Somewhere along the way we have substituted faithfulness to Christ with worldly versions of success that are measured only by numbers. Please don't get me wrong, I have a tremendous appreciation for good research that helps us all make better choices about how we help others. As my friend Albert Loewen says, Jesus was primarily concerned with doing God's will, whatever that may be. Instead of being obsessed with saving the world, let us be obsessed with Jesus, the one we are told to imitate and the one who is "the image of the invisible God" (Colossians 1:15). Following Jesus into the will of God through the power of the Holy Spirit should be our great and magnificent obsession—like my friend Joe in Edmonton who had to take a moment to simply revel in his love for his Savior at the mere mention of his name.

THREE

The Revelation of Your Hidden Beliefs

THE MAN SAT IN MY STUDY and talked about how much he had changed. He spoke of how he had confessed his sins and was a different man now; he spoke with great fervor and even with tears. I didn't believe him, which of course sounds callous and jaded. I had lost count of how many times this same man sat in my study making these same claims. After each conversation, I would pray with him and urge him to prove his claims by living them out, then he would leave and go back to his family. Sometimes it was only hours until more conflict erupted because of his . . . well . . . lapses in judgment. On a few occasions, emergency services got involved. I suspect that most pastors have dealt with someone like this at some point, and I have watched situations like this play out repeatedly in different places and ways throughout my years in ministry. When someone's words are so drastically inconsistent with their actions, I come to question the veracity of their claims. In fact, there are times where it would be foolish and negligent to accept someone's words at face value.

What we say we believe and what we truly believe are not always the same thing. Sometimes we are consciously aware of these differences, and other times we seem to stumble into situations where our words and actions do not align. Add to that humanity's tremendous capacity for self-deception, and being a person of integrity becomes an increasingly large task for anyone. Philosopher Søren Kierkegaard put it this way, "The matter is quite simple. The Bible is very easy to understand. But we Christians are a bunch of scheming swindlers. We pretend to be unable to understand it because we know very well that the minute we understand, we are obligated to act accordingly. Take any words in the New Testament and forget everything except pledging yourself to act accordingly."[1] I need look no further than a mirror to discover that my own actions do not line up with my own ideals, professed beliefs, or the teachings of Jesus. To borrow the language of Bryant Myers, my life is a witness that is always testifying to what I actually believe. When it comes to the topic of poverty and what we can or should do to reduce it, there are a couple of ways that we Christians miss the mark and end up being witnesses that testify to something different from what our words would claim.

On one hand, Christians sometimes claim to care about helping others and serving those on the margins of society but simply don't do it. Helping the poor becomes something we like to talk about but never do; it is a favorite discussion topic so long as it remains in the realm of discussion. We would rather live selfishly than actually do the work of converting our words and ideals into tangible actions, revealing that we don't actually care about this belief, at least not enough to actually do something about it.

Conversely, we can fall into a frame of mind that judges and condemns others who don't do as much as we think they should. While we may or may not be accurate in an assessment of someone else's ability to do more, driving wedges into the Christian community and polarizing our churches is not inspiring nor helpful if we actually want to make a difference. Sharp rebukes have their place, but the way of Jesus is one marked by love and not hatred. One common way we may do this is to despise anyone with more wealth than us, placing a large amount of blame on them for the problems we see in the world. We can become cynical peddlers of blame and shame, living as legalistic Christians who forget about concepts like grace and mercy.

Let's look at our first pitfall. James, the brother of Jesus, wrote, "Do not merely listen to the word, and so deceive yourselves. Do what it says" (James 1:22). Given that this was written so long ago, it stands to reason that even early Christians struggled with living out their faith, and finding justifications for not doing what they knew they were supposed to be doing. This is an ongoing theme in the book of James, which even goes so far as to say, "If anyone, then, knows the good they ought to do and doesn't do it, it is sin for them" (James 4:17), and that "faith without deeds is dead" (James 2:26). While this may be difficult for us to wrestle with, wrestle with it we must. It can be a scary prospect, because when we begin such a journey we don't always know where we will end up. We wrestle with following Jesus because it calls us to something more than we are, and so we sometimes in turn struggle with who God is—in part because we would rather have a god made in our image than follow the God in whose image we are made. Gary Haugen, the founder of International Justice Mission, writes, "Acknowledging that we are struggling with what the Bible teaches about the character of God is often the first, best step to authentic faith. Indeed, as Dallas Willard points out in *Renovation of the Heart*, 'we don't believe something by merely saying we believe it, or even when we believe that we believe it. We believe something when we act as if it were true.'"[2] Pastor Bruxy Cavey puts it this way, "Faith from a biblical point of view is active trust. It's trusting in a person enough to follow after them, to listen to what they say, and if we believe Jesus is Lord, then our faith in Christ should be reflected in how we live, not just in what we say we believe."[3]

In Matthew 25, Jesus tells a parable about how, at the final judgment, God will separate the sheep from the goats, with the sheep entering into eternal life and the goats into eternal punishment. The sheep were the ones who gave water to those who were thirsty, showed hospitality to strangers, clothed the naked, looked after the sick, or visited those in prison. The goats did none of these things, and Jesus tells us that "whatever you did for one of the least of these brothers and sisters of mine, you did for me" (Matthew 25:40). This is a bold statement, and together with the passages from James becomes a sobering reminder about how we should live. I must admit that this passage makes me uncomfortable, especially when read on its own because it can sound like salvation is based only on our works. Our salvation, however, is certainly based on the grace of God and the perfect work of Jesus. Bible commentator Leon Morris puts it this way,

> We must bear in mind that this picture of Judgment Day does not give us a full account of everything that has to do with salvation; it does not include, for example, the fact that from the beginning of his Gospel Matthew has been writing about one who will "save his people from their sins" (1:21; cf. also 11:25-30; 20:28). This passage deals with the evidence on which people will be judged, not the cause of salvation or damnation. That grace is not part of the present picture does not mean it is any less significant. We must bear in mind that it is common to the whole scriptural picture that we are saved by grace and judged by works. The works we do are the evidence either of the grace of God at work in us or of our rejection of that grace."[4]

Nonetheless, these passages do present us with a very strong imperative not to leave our faith merely in the realm of thinking or discussion, but to live it out in concrete ways.

Shane Claiborne has said, "As I look at the challenge in the church I don't think our challenge is right thinking, but it's right living. I think we've got a lot of the ideas, we've even got a lot of the theology that's there, and yet it doesn't always translate into action." Claiborne also presents a possibility for how this comes to be, suggesting that there are many instances where people don't live out their faith in regard to helping those in material poverty because they don't personally know many people experiencing it. Our society makes it easy to isolate ourselves from others, which is a barrier both to meaningful community and to everyday encounters where people can forge friendships. As Claiborne has said, "It's not that we don't care, it's that we don't know where to start. . . . One of the real problems in the church is *not* that wealthy folks don't care about the poor but that wealthy folks don't know the poor. Part of what we do is we compartmentalize service and charity in ways that we provide programs and money but we don't actually have a lot of transformative relationships." [5] Finding ways to actually build these kinds of relationships is vitally important (more on that in chapter 10). While we may have good motives or intentions, the message that our lack of action communicates is less than inspiring, and overcoming this pitfall requires intentionality.

When you examine your life, do you find yourself merely talking about caring for others, or are you actively living out the gospel? Is your faith mostly limited to words, or is it being translated into action? What messages or beliefs is your life testifying to? If you honestly answer this question and find yourself lacking, you might feel guilty or ashamed or disheartened; but take courage, because you now have a chance to do better. Or perhaps as you read this you know that your life is full of actions, and you are giving a hearty "Amen" to some of these rebukes to the church that call us out of a state of complacency and proverbial slumber. If this is you, then I am happy to see you translating your beliefs into actions that help others; but before you get too exuberant, let's discuss another pitfall that is easy to fall into.

While some of us fail to follow Jesus by not being obedient to his teachings, others of us fail by attempting to take his place. Jesus, and not us, is the ruler and savior of the world. While the church is tasked with partnering with Jesus in the mission of God, it is not *we* who are meant to save the world. Unfortunately, this understanding is sometimes missing as we talk about reducing poverty. There is so much poverty and suffering in the world, and we truly have much work to do. We can get so overzealous, however, that we start to usurp the place of Jesus, and instead of being one part of Christ's body, we take on the responsibility to save the whole world. We then often become judgmental of others who are not doing as much, and our actions can very easily become devoid of God's mercy, grace, and love. As the apostle Paul writes, "If I give all I possess to the poor and give over my body to hardship that I may boast, but do not have love, I gain nothing" (1 Corinthians 13:3).

Mark Galli, the former editor in chief of *Christianity Today*, touches on this very concept when he says, "The American church, and the evangelical church in particular, has let our activism in the name of God eclipse our passion for God."[6] This isn't exactly a new concept, but it is one that is increasingly relevant to the church. C. S. Lewis wrote about people "who got so interested in proving the existence of God that they came to care nothing for God himself . . . as if the good Lord had nothing to do but to exist. There have been some who were so preoccupied with spreading Christianity that they never gave a thought to Christ."[7]

I suspect that many of us who fall victim to this pitfall do so because somewhere deep down we believe that we must earn

God's approval and earn our place in heaven, though we likely wouldn't verbalize such a thought. We minimize the importance of the grace of God—sometimes even losing sight of the person of God—and instead focus on doing more and achieving more. To use a biblical illustration from Luke 10, we become like Martha and judge those like Mary. While Mary was spending time listening to Jesus teach, her sister Martha was busy hosting and serving, and she wanted Mary's help. Eventually Martha asked Jesus to tell Mary to stop being so lazy and to help with the work. Instead of sending Mary to help, Jesus replied, "Martha, Martha, . . . you are worried and upset about many things, but few things are needed—or indeed only one. Mary has chosen what is better, and it will not be taken away from her" (Luke 10:41-42). Jesus wasn't about to pass judgment on Mary because her expression of devotion looked different from Martha's.

I must admit that I am more prone to this pitfall than to the error of complacency. As I have examined this in my own life, I have come to realize that working harder and doing more is one way I sometimes seek to control the outcome of my life, or control how other people see me, or control how I feel about myself. This led me to a rather startling realization: this is idolatry. I am seeking to control my own life by offering my efforts to gain the approval of others, instead of seeking to gain the approval of the one true God. Instead of giving my anxious thoughts and uneasiness about our world's imperfections to my Savior, I try to become the savior of the world by working harder. Don't get me wrong, working hard can be a very good thing, but it can also be a way we seek to control things that are best left up to God. Consider the idolatry we read about in the Old Testament. People fell into the trap of idolatry because they were told that the solution to one's problems was to follow the correct ritual to honor the correct deity, who would solve the problems. For instance, folks who struggled with infertility would make sacrifices to the fertility gods, seeking to improve their lot and take control of their own fate by abandoning the God of Israel and serving another god that promised to give them what they wanted—if only they would make the correct sacrifice. If we are trying to help others in order to control the way people see us, the way we feel about ourselves, or how God sees us, we are no longer following Jesus—instead we are asking Jesus to follow us, usurping his role as ruler and Savior. If we try to reduce or eliminate poverty because we believe it is our place to save the world and we try to use Jesus to help us achieve our goals, we put ourselves in Jesus' place.

This can be a very subtle shift in perspective, yet the subtle errors are often the most damaging. Consider the Old Testament story of Joshua. God was going to give the people of Israel the Promised Land. They were entering the land at God's command, and then Joshua had an interesting encounter with a spiritual being who ended up being the commander of the Lord's armies. Joshua asked if this person was on Israel's side or the side of their enemies. The being responded by saying, "Neither" (Joshua 5:14). What the being meant was that he was on God's side, not Israel's nor Jericho's. He was reminding Joshua that God wasn't there to do Israel's bidding and achieve Israel's goals, and he was inviting Joshua and Israel to submit to the Lord and follow God. In this instance, the short-term goals of God and Israel aligned. In the long term, however, the consequences of serving themselves would be devastating, as eventually became clear in Israel's history. I remain convinced that Jesus desires us to live out our faith by helping others, but I also believe that we ought to remember our place before God.

Instead of pointing others to Jesus in both word and deed, the content of our lives may sometimes point others to ourselves and our own good deeds. Other times we may make fools of ourselves, our actions testifying to our own selfishness, complacency, or even ignorance. We may testify to our unspoken belief that our lives are more important than others, or we may reveal that we actually believe God will not accept us unless we do enough good things. As Myers says, "There is no such thing as not witnessing. . . . The only question is to whom or to what?"[8]

I don't believe the question is whether or not we live out our faith in the way that we should. I have yet to meet anyone who does this perfectly. The question instead is this: What area of our lives do we need to better align with what we claim to believe? While an examination of our lives may reveal hypocrisy within our hearts, do not be discouraged. In the words of theologian Stanley Hauerwas, "The fact that we have often been less than we were meant to be should never be used as an excuse for shirking the task of being the people of God."[9] Do not give up on living out your beliefs just because you have failed to do so in the past. Greg Pearson, who works at an inner-city ministry in Saskatchewan, puts it this way, "The way I define integrity is this: it's the ability to wake up every morning and try to narrow the gap between what I say and what I do."[10]

While you might be tempted to make a mental checklist of your best attributes and actions right now, instead consider this: In your worst moments of, say, the past week, what does the witness of your life testify to? Considering our best moments might help us to feel better, but considering our worst moments is more helpful for us to grow. As we consider the ways in which our actions betray our faulty unspoken beliefs, we come face-to-face with the difficult notion that we are incredibly broken. Thankfully, in God's kingdom, being broken isn't a bad place to be if we want to authentically follow after Jesus.

FOUR

Broken

IT WAS A VERY DIFFICULT TIME in my life. I had been treated unjustly, in ways that had left me deeply hurt. In the aftermath of this experience, I met weekly with my pastor, Pete, who listened compassionately and was truly present in my pain. Pete acknowledged how deeply I was wronged and prayed with me and for me, trying to help me find healing. After a couple of months of weekly meetings, Pete shared a story with me. That was often how Pete shared important truths—not by speaking the truths directly but by sharing a story that would illustrate the point he wanted to make. It was one of many ways that Pastor Pete reminded me of Jesus. Pete told me a story of a time he had been wronged and had held on to his anger long after the troubling event had been resolved. He shared how he'd become so accustomed to being outraged that over time he began to express anger at minor infractions by those in his life whom he cared about most. Pete told me that he found that he had to let go of his right to outrage in order to move forward. I had known Pete for years, and I knew him well enough to understand what he was saying.

I was letting my moral outrage consume me. I was walking not the road to healing but the road to perpetual victimhood. Pete's story was a warning that I could end up damaging my marriage and family, exaggerating my victim status when my loved ones made small mistakes and then using that as justification to hurt them in return. I was at risk of becoming a living example of the old adage "Hurt people hurt people." I was hurt, and if I continued down the path I was on, I might end up repeating the cycle, creating more hurt people.

The content of my life during those months communicated that I believed I wouldn't find healing until the wrongs were righted, although I never would have stated it as such at the time. I didn't stay and chat very long after Pete told me that story, and I left his office very upset. How could Pete suggest that *I* needed to change? How dare he suggest that I let go of my desire for *justice*! Didn't he care? I knew very well that he did, but I still *felt* betrayed. On the way home from this meeting, a song came on my stereo whose lyrics were providential. The song also told a story, one of how the singer was pursuing particular goals at the expense of his family. My mind went to my wife and newborn baby. Was I leaving them hungry for love because I was so consumed with receiving some kind of acknowledgment of wrongdoing from the people who had hurt me? My heart softened, and I began to see that if I didn't stop chasing after something that I could never actually have, I would end up hurting those closest to me. Yes, I wanted justice, but I was not in any position to get it, and it was little more than a pipe dream. I could see that I had already left my wife hungry for my affection and love because I was so consumed with my own pain. If I didn't change my direction, I would become the bad guy in the story of her life, the one hurting her and leaving my whole family in pain. That day I came face-to-face not only with the brokenness of my own hurts and pains, but also with my own propensity to hurt others.

The next week I showed up again at Pete's office. He said, "I didn't know if you would be back." Pete took a risk in sharing that story with me. He could wisely see that the path I was going down was heading to endless despair, and he wanted to help me find healing instead of further devastation. He risked our friendship that day, and he knew it, and I will always be thankful to God that he did. It was as if Pete held up a mirror to me to help me see who I was becoming. While I despised what I saw, I needed to be shown the depths of my own brokenness if I were to have any hope of finding healing. If I didn't take responsibility for my own healing, even while facing tremendous injustice, I would surely perpetuate further injustice. I could see that this had already begun in subtle ways. I had known that I had been wronged, but now I also recognized that I was turning into someone who could continue to hurt others just as I had been hurt. This was a truly humbling realization, and the picture I had of myself changed from a justice warrior to an unpleasant, bitter, and entitled child. My distorted view of myself became more realistic, and I no longer liked what I saw. This changed the direction of our conversations, and trusty ol' Pastor Pete helped me set a better trajectory for my life and marriage, and helped me find healing.

Perhaps you are like me, and don't always like what you see when you examine your own life. It is easier to see and critique the wrongs of others than to take a good long look in the mirror to discover our own faults. When we do this—when we evaluate ourselves with sober judgment, not thinking of ourselves more highly than we ought—we begin to come to grips with the depths of our own sinfulness and how dreadfully inadequate we are. Through this experience, and many others like it, I came to see again exactly why the gospel is so offensive. In the midst of a broken world, with all kinds of tragedy, suffering, and injustice all around us, in order to find healing we must recognize our own sinfulness and our own need for a Savior. While the transformation that Christ offers does in fact bring us healing, and while God compassionately walks with us in our hurts, this is not possible without recognizing our own brokenness, sinfulness, and need for salvation.

In the book of Romans, Paul writes, "I would not have known what sin was had it not been for the law" (Romans 7:7). God gives us the law, and it shows us, like a mirror, how sinful we really are. It reminds us that "all have sinned and fall short of the glory of God" (Romans 3:23). This is precisely one of the reasons why Jesus came, so that even though we have sinned and have experienced tremendous brokenness and feel dead inside, we can be made alive with Christ (Ephesians 2:5).

If we accept the idea that the root cause of poverty is a series of broken relationships, then we can begin to move from seeing poverty as something *out there* to something that we all struggle with in some way. The nuances and complexities begin to make more sense. The problems become less theoretical and more personal. If we seek to reduce poverty by helping bring healing to broken relationships, then we can ask ourselves a revealing question: What would it take to heal all the broken relationships in my life? What would it take for me to have a healthy relationship with God? What would it take to mend the broken relationships between myself and others? What would it take to heal the destructive thought patterns that I have when I think about myself? What would it take for me to have a healthy relationship with my environment? My guess is that your answer to those questions would be lengthy, with many layers and complexities and few if any clear-cut and simple solutions. The same is true for broken relationships that cause material poverty, which is what makes addressing it so difficult. As we consider the difficulty of healing broken relationships, as we consider our own difficulty in living out the teachings of Jesus, and as we examine our own hypocrisy, there are few words as fitting as the words from Psalm 86:3, "Have mercy on me, Lord, for I call to you all day long."

We read in the book of Micah, "He has shown you, O mortal, what is good. And what does the LORD require of you? To act justly and to love mercy and to walk humbly with your God" (Micah 6:8). This is an important passage in such discussions and gives us some very important principles to live by. The first part is to act justly. We generally want others to treat us justly, and it makes sense that the Bible would call us to just living. Yet as I already discussed, there are times when achieving true justice is out of our control. Thankfully, the Bible gives us commands to act justly and to seek justice, but it doesn't command us to guarantee the outcome—that ultimately is left up to God, who will in the end make all things right. The prophet Isaiah tells us, "Learn to do right; seek justice. Defend the oppressed. Take up the cause of the fatherless; plead the case of the widow" (Isaiah 1:17). While we learn to act more justly and to seek justice, however, we should not neglect our love for mercy, because mercy is something we all desperately need.

The word for mercy in this passage in Micah is the Hebrew word *chesed*. It can mean steadfast love, mercy, loyalty, or kindness. Some scholars talk about chesed as meaning "maintaining a faithful covenant relationship."[1] This is partly why efforts that seek to feed the hungry or heal the sick or care for the orphaned are called mercy ministries. Chesed encompasses acts of compassion and service, it includes aspects of grace and forgiveness, and it is a word that holistically describes the way we ought to live in a covenant relationship with our Creator. Yet as is the case with many things, we also offer to others what God offers us. We receive the blessings of God and then are asked to offer those same blessings to others. In this case we ought to treat others with the same chesed that God has shown us. And while we must be committed to acting justly, there are times when we cannot achieve justice. So we love chesed. We love the covenant relationship that we have with God. This relationship is what we need more than anything. This kind of mercy, or chesed, is that which our souls need to breathe, and it is incredibly important for the Christian life. It becomes what motivates us to love and serve others, and it is also what restores us when we fail. Far too often when we talk about reducing poverty, we writers and preachers proverbially beat people over the head as we deliver our messages. While there may be truth in these rebukes, it is also important that in our zeal to encourage Christians to show chesed to the world, we don't neglect to show that same chesed to one another.

This is more than just a bandwagon mentality. This is deeper than just another social movement. It's not just more rhetoric to get more people to open their wallets to charities or propaganda to guilt us into doing more. Mercy, or chesed, is a deep-seated need within our very soul. Without mercy there is no hope of healing for broken relationships, not with God, with others, or within ourselves. Without chesed we are stuck in an endless cycle of giving and receiving pain. Justice without mercy leaves us without a life-giving relationship with God, who is the very reason we seek justice in the first place. And mercy without acting justly is an inherent contradiction.

So I invite you to come back once again to Jesus. After he called Matthew—who, as a tax collector, was a social outcast among the religious elite—to be his disciple, Jesus attended a dinner at Matthew's home. The teachers of the religious law saw that Jesus was eating with sinners and asked why he would dare do such a thing. Jesus responded by saying, "It is not the healthy who need a doctor, but the sick. But go and learn what this means: 'I desire mercy, not sacrifice.' For I have not come to call the righteous, but sinners" (Matthew 9:12-13). Though you may be broken, it is you for whom Jesus came. Though you may be a great sinner, Jesus came to offer you chesed. It was the sinners whom Jesus called to be his disciples—it isn't that the religious leaders weren't sinners, it was that they didn't recognize the sin that was staring them in the face. If you have come to recognize your own brokenness and even sinfulness, there is good news for you because Jesus is offering you mercy. It is you whom Jesus is calling into his service. It is you to whom he wants to show mercy so that you might have the power to extend mercy to all your relationships. Your brokenness does not disqualify you from being a follower of Jesus. As God told the apostle Paul, "My grace is sufficient for you, for my power is made perfect in weakness" (2 Corinthians 12:9). Your ability to serve God is not dependent on your own perfection, and your brokenness is where you just might most clearly see God at work.

God uses broken people to achieve the purposes of the divine. Catholic priest and writer Henri Nouwen, in *The Wounded Healer*, emphasizes that God does not work through us despite our wounds, but precisely because of them. Nouwen writes, "It is an illusion to think that a person can be led out of the desert by someone who has never been there."[2] I don't believe the question is whether we are broken people, but rather whether we have discovered our own brokenness yet. If we have, then we need to ask whether we have come to Jesus for hope and for healing. As we work to serve others, we will be tempted to position ourselves as the experts—the ones with all the answers who know what to do, where to go, and how to get there. Yet Nouwen writes powerfully about the mysterious ways of God, who often throughout history has worked through the broken and disenfranchised.

Consider Bible characters like Gideon, who was, in today's terms, a nobody—yet God used Gideon to save a nation. It was a despised slave child named Moses who grew up to challenge an empire and lead God's people out of slavery. The apostle Paul says that "God chose the foolish things of the world to shame the wise; God chose the weak things of the world to shame the strong" (1 Corinthians 1:27). There are countless times when God works in ways we would not expect, and in ways that we might call foolish. The things that seem to be a waste of time may end up being the most worthwhile things. If you see in yourself all kinds of brokenness, then you are in good company because God has used countless people like you to make a big difference in the world.

But before we let this get to our heads, we must also consider another important part of the Micah 6 passage. After talking about justice and mercy, the last part of verse 8 gives us more than just a hint as to the disposition we ought to have as we seek to follow the Lord: "walk humbly with your God." And so we must. The importance of humility cannot be overstated. Without humility we won't recognize our own brokenness and therefore won't be able to properly receive healing. Without humility we will think we are too good to do those things that God is asking us to do. Without humility we may not be willing to start doing the small, seemingly insignificant things that are of utmost importance in the life of the Christian. Humility is more than a little important in helping us become the people we are meant to be. (More on this in chapter 7.)

So may we act justly and seek justice. May we love mercy and extend it freely in our relationships with one another, living in covenant faithfulness to our Lord. And may we walk humbly with God as we make our way in this world, being the hands and feet of Jesus, even as God is still at work bringing healing to our deepest wounds and our own profound brokenness.

PART 2: **Understanding Poverty**

My philosophy professor in university, Hendrik van der Breggen, is known for often saying, "Ideas have consequences." He is right. The way we think affects what we do, how we behave, and thus the impact we have in the world. Jesus said, "A good man brings good things out of the good stored up in his heart, and an evil man brings evil things out of the evil stored up in his heart. For the mouth speaks what the heart is full of" (Luke 6:45). The way we think about poverty changes how we respond and can result in doing greater harm or greater good. We need to remember that poverty is not just an interesting topic of discussion, but something that affects people with names and faces. We also need to reflect on our approach to it, our attitudes, and some of the complicating factors like addictions and mental illness. Furthermore, we need to remember to take care of ourselves even as we seek to help care for others. In this section I will challenge some prevalent ways of thinking about poverty and bring a few things to our attention that are important in the work of reducing and eliminating poverty in our world.

FIVE

They Have Faces and Names

SOME TIME AGO, I was attending a church breakfast in my role as a pastor when the people around me began swapping stories about their younger years, and the topic turned to experiences with bullies in school. At some point I shared a story about some of the people who bullied me, then made an off-hand remark that disparagingly referred to them as "dropouts" because they never finished high school. At first, I thought nothing of it and moved on with my day. But later I was taken aside and confronted about my comments. You see, what I did in that moment was alienate most of the people around me, because most of them had never been able to finish high school. They were "dropouts" themselves, and it took only one word to inflict damage. When they were fairly young, they were forced to enter the workforce in order to help take care of their families. Their families suffered from such severe poverty that continuing their education was not a viable option and their efforts were required to help provide the basic necessities. I was not only unkind to those who had bullied me by speaking badly about them, but I had referred to dropping out of high school as if it were an indicator of having a substandard character, insulting those around me and hurting our relationships. I revealed my ignorance about the many reasons for being unable to finish high school and made those around me feel as if I viewed them as less valuable than those of us who did graduate. While this was not my intention, my motives were irrelevant because of the damage done by my reckless words.

When we talk about poverty, we often discuss theories and frameworks, principles and paradigms. What we sometimes forget, however, is that there would be no poverty without people. We are talking about human beings. They have faces, names, and stories. As Christians, we believe all humanity is made in the image of God, and therefore worthy of inherent dignity and respect. Yet it is in this very discussion about poverty, which is often motivated by a desire to *help* people, where we can lose sight of the fact that we are talking about human beings. Countless times I have heard people do exactly what I did: speak insensitively about poverty, not realizing that in a single moment one can effectively alienate individuals and even entire communities.

Sometimes when we talk about poverty in ways that are insensitive, we make insulting remarks about others that, instead of revealing something bad about *them*, reveal something broken within *ourselves*. Consider the well-documented story of the late Canadian politician Ralph Klein, who stopped at a homeless shelter to berate its guests in a slurred rant, telling them to get jobs and even throwing change at them.[1] "King Ralph," as he was affectionately called in Alberta, did give the public a kind of revelation—not so much about those who are homeless but about him. After this incident, he publicly acknowledged his own struggle with alcohol, revealing a poverty in himself that is just as serious as that which afflicts those who deal with homelessness. While he was arguably the most powerful man in the province, this incident revealed the truth that he was just as broken as those who bore the brunt of his scorn.[2]

One of the most effective ways to transform our discussions about poverty in this regard is to humanize the discussion—to hear the stories of those who have dealt with poverty and to build relationships with them. Here are a few stories of real people who have experienced poverty firsthand.[3]

Sharon was a single mother who was receiving social assistance. She got a part-time job because she wanted to work to support herself and her child. Somewhere along the way, her son was diagnosed with Type 1 diabetes, and was in need of regular insulin injections just to survive. These were incredibly expensive. Thankfully, the social assistance program she was a part of paid for those medical expenses. As she began to work more, she came to a difficult realization: if she worked thirty or more hours a week, she would lose her placement in the welfare program entirely, which meant she would have to pay for the expensive medical needs of her son. Yet her basic needs, without considering her son's medical costs, required that she work more than thirty hours each week. The transition from social assistance to self-sustaining work was so harsh that she wasn't able to do it without placing her son's health and life in jeopardy. She had to choose between her desire to be independent and self-sufficient and the health of her son. Sharon wasn't lazy, but the institutional systems in which she existed made it impossible for her to transition to self-sustaining work without risking her son's health while she did so. If the system would have allowed her to keep the medical assistance until she worked her way to getting more hours or found a job with benefits, then she could have eventually come off social assistance entirely. Thanks to the system's lack of flexibility, however, she had to remain on welfare indefinitely. If you were a parent in that situation, what would you do?

Sometimes the systems and institutions that are in place to help people in poverty end up keeping them in poverty, people like Sharon and countless others like her. In these situations, the transition out of poverty is an impossible one, and while people aren't lazy and want to work, they must also consider the well-being of their children in order to be responsible parents. Yet people call them "welfare bums," and they are told to just work harder, when that isn't the root of or even remotely relevant to their problem. If we speak in such a way, we only reveal our own ignorance instead of adding anything meaningful to the conversation or to the relationship.

Patrick was the first in his family to graduate high school. None of his aunts, uncles, cousins, or siblings had graduated, but he did. There was a catch, however: Patrick was mostly illiterate. He had been pushed through the system, grade after grade, without being taught how to read properly. He was from a single-parent family that struggled to get by, and there was even a time when he and his family lived in a shelter after they were forced from their home. The education system had failed him, and he was left to enter the workforce at a severe disadvantage. When he struggled with reading in the younger grades, rather than give him extra time to help him learn to read, his school just passed him on to the next teacher, hoping they could fix the problem. This happened repeatedly until he was a young adult ready to graduate. While he had his high school diploma, which would improve his odds of finding gainful employment, he would be at a severe disadvantage as to the kinds of jobs for which he could apply. He needed help even to fill out the paperwork required to apply for a job. While Patrick's story doesn't end badly—he did find work he enjoys and is doing quite well—many experience less fortunate outcomes because of being pushed through the education system rather than being educated.

Susan was a young professional who became an alcoholic in her mid-twenties. Her addiction grew worse until she eventually lost her job and went on welfare. She had a daughter whom she cared for, and for the sake of herself and her daughter she fought hard to achieve sobriety, successfully completing her rehabilitation program. When I met Susan, she had been sober for almost a decade and had managed to transition off social assistance. She spoke of the poverty of her past and how one of her major challenges had been dietary. When she was beginning to work again, but was not yet back to being entirely self-sufficient, money was very tight and it was hard to pay the bills. Since it can be expensive to buy vegetables and leafy greens, she would often buy boxes of macaroni and cheese or other inexpensive but less healthy foods. With such an unhealthy diet, she and her daughter became much more susceptible to the flu and colds, causing Susan to miss work because she was ill so often. This led to less income, which led to an even worse diet. Susan spoke about experiencing depression and that overcoming it included eating a healthy diet, which in previous years she had not been able to afford.

Susan's all too common story illustrates the spirals of negative reinforcement that so many people in poverty experience. For Susan, not being able to afford to eat a healthy diet led to getting sick more often and missing work, which in turn led to even poorer health and even more missed work, and so the downward spiral continued. This is just one example, but many different factors can result in a negative spiral of events, like an undercurrent sweeping a person down to a dark and dangerous place. Several spirals can take place in one person's life all at once, and the complete explanation becomes complex and multifaceted. These negative spirals also have psychological consequences. As they go through life and meet others who seem to have their lives together, with one good thing followed by another, people like Susan can begin to feel inferior, perhaps even wondering if God has cursed them or abandoned them to the misery of their poverty. People like Susan can begin to have a distorted view of their own value, and may believe that their life isn't as valuable as the lives of those who are wealthy. This kind of mentality never has positive outcomes. This negative mentality is so common that development professionals have a term for it: the "marred identity of the poor."[4] Bryant Myers calls it a broken relationship with oneself. When someone believes their state of poverty is a key piece of their identity, that adds to the spirals of negative reinforcement in their life. Instead of viewing their poverty as something *external* to who they are, it becomes a reality that they believe stems *from* who they are. While that may seem like a small distinction, the implications are far-reaching. (More on this in chapter 7.)

Just as people in poverty often experience spirals of negative reinforcement, some of us experience spirals of positive reinforcement. As a very simple example, consider the many businesspeople who have company credit cards that collect points which can be exchanged for flights. Since a lot of cash flow goes through those accounts, they quickly accumulate free flights and are then able to afford exciting vacations. These vacations are virtually free and help the business owner disconnect from their toil, have fun, enjoy the good things of life, and improve their mental health. This in turn helps them come back to work refreshed and ready to work at growing their company, which creates more wealth and more benefits for themselves. And so the positive spiral continues. Or think of what would happen in the reverse of Susan's situation: the investment of eating healthy food leads to less sickness and fewer missed work days, which results in more income and a greater ability to afford to eat a healthy diet.

Our family has talked a lot about these spirals of positive reinforcement recently. When my wife returned to the workforce and began working full-time, her employer provided our family with medical, dental, and other health-related benefits. Now she was working more hours, getting a higher wage, and receiving benefits. We had more money in our pockets, and our medical expenses cost less. Though we are now better able to afford to pay full price for prescriptions and glasses, we don't have to. It feels like the system was built so that the moment we had more money, things cost us less, leaving us with even more money in our pockets.

There was a time in my life when I was dreadfully jealous of people who were experiencing these spirals of positive reinforcement. My jealousy led to resentment, and I viewed the situation as unfair, which led to a sense of entitlement as well. The reality is that the people I knew and had resented because they seemed to have easy lives didn't necessarily choose their paths, and they weren't immoral people because of it. In fact, many of them gave even more generously to others because of their own success. Just as people don't inherently have greater character because they experience spirals of negative reinforcement, so too people don't inherently have lesser character because they experience spirals of positive reinforcement, and vice versa.

While our systems can be just and good, sometimes our institutions and societies are designed so that certain people groups experience more spirals of negative reinforcement than the rest of society—and that is unjust. Sometimes institutionalized policies result in certain people groups experiencing more spirals of positive reinforcement than others. While these systems may at times be unjust and immoral, it does not mean that those I envied were necessarily unjust and immoral. It was eye-opening for me to realize, however, that envy *is* a sin and is, by definition, immoral. And the jealousy I nurtured only resulted in further spirals of negative reinforcement in my life, because it led to bitterness, making it more difficult for me to be thankful for what I did have. My resentment also hindered relationships that would have otherwise enriched my experience of community, leading to a greater sense of social isolation, which wasn't helpful for emotional or mental health, and impacted the levels of happiness I experienced.

While the systems that favor some people over others may be unjust, I have come to realize that those I was jealous of often had no more control over societal systems than I did. Just as they couldn't control which social group they were born into, neither could I control which social group I was born into. So while I had to work much harder to begin experiencing spirals of positive reinforcement, I found that some of those whom I had previously been jealous of and resented became powerful allies and influences in my journey to creating a better life for myself and breaking cycles of poverty. They were compassionate and generous, and resented unjust systems just as much as I did. They were just as clueless as I was about how to change things in our world. But they wanted to do what they could. I have come to believe that we should follow in the example of some of my friends, who work creatively at helping people escape from spirals of negative reinforcement, and help individuals discover how to overcome negative paths and discover spirals of positive reinforcement. While some systems of positive and negative reinforcement are of our own making, there are countless times when they are not. Judging and condemning those experiencing negative spirals—or being jealous of those experiencing positive ones—is not helpful, moral, or just. All these people are just that: people. They are all made in God's image and deserving of dignity and respect.

While there are things we can do together to help change the systems that can keep people in poverty, we must not lose sight of the fact that we are talking about people. We must not dehumanize others or use them simply to advance our own ideas about what is needed. This has happened and continues to happen to Indigenous people in Canada, when governments and individuals in power make decisions on behalf of communities without involving them. This approach has repeatedly resulted in greater poverty. My friend Kyle Mason is an Ojibway/Métis leader, and he puts it like this, "Nothing for us, without us." [5]

Whether we are discussing the reasons why people are in poverty, or whether we are trying to help reduce it, we must not forget the humanity of those we are talking about. We must not forget about the Sharons and the Patricks and the Susans of this world, must not judge them without knowing them, or decide their fate without including them.

It is far too easy to communicate in word or in deed in a way that alienates others. Even if that is not our intention, we may, as I did when recounting a tale of a childhood bully, end up alienating those with whom we seek to build relationships. The ease with which this occurs is telling, and should be a stark warning to heed the advice of James: "Everyone should be quick to listen, slow to speak and slow to become angry" (James 1:19).

SIX

The Good News

WHEN I WAS A CHILD, my family and I were considered the "working poor." There were many in our world poorer than us, and since my dad always worked, I never had to go to bed with an empty stomach. We were never forced to sleep outside, because even when we lost our home when I was eight years old, we had family who took us in. From before I was born, my parents helped people who had nowhere to go, and we had a great many houseguests, some staying for days or weeks, and others staying for months or years. I know what it is like to go without a telephone (that was rather nice, actually), there was a season when we went without indoor plumbing, and for years of my upbringing the only heat in our home through the bitter cold Canadian winters was from a woodstove. We would glean firewood from woodpiles at the local lumber mills that were destined for the burner as waste, cutting up the bent and splintered logs in the evenings and on weekends. No matter how bad things got, however, we never had to go without food, we had clothes on our backs, and I was keenly aware that we were more privileged than others because of how often we would encounter people in need, people who were always welcome in our home and around our table.

We always went to church, and I knew my parents had a deep love for Jesus. It was clear to me that their hospitality was an out-working of their faith, and despite their failures, they did their best to help others, and this was my "normal." While there was lots of talk about the Bible, Jesus, and faith in general, my parents didn't talk much about "helping the poor" or about "social justice." They just did it. We didn't help out at soup kitchens or volunteer at homeless shelters. We didn't participate in big fund-raisers for nonprofits. My parents' ministry service was largely to simply let people in, and to spend time with them around our dinner table, in our living room, and on the front porch. It seemed like our home was always being used to help someone. As a teenager there were several times when our friends had no-where to go, so we brought them home with us, and my parents always let them stay as long as they needed. I had no idea that this was an abnormal way to live; while I didn't see many others living this way, I never felt self-conscious about this way of life. Little did I know that talking about this would be extremely con-troversial to some people. I had never even heard about the term *social gospel* until after my wife and I got married.

Imagine my surprise to discover that some people get up-set at the idea of helping others, arguing that we should only tell others about Jesus because that is supposedly all that they need. While I knew that humanity needed Jesus, I had met plenty of people who also needed a good meal and a roof over their heads for a while. Many of these people became my room-mates. Furthermore, my family and I had been those people. I was surprised again to learn that others would get upset about the idea of talking about Jesus instead of just giving food, cloth-ing, and shelter. In our home, regardless of whether other peo-ple were there, there was often talk about Jesus and the gospel.

While receiving a meal was in no way contingent on becoming a Christian or listening to such talk, the concept of separating our faith from sharing our food seemed foreign and strange. I was offended at the idea that my family should hide who we were as people of faith if others in need of food and a place to sleep came over. I was also offended at the idea of telling someone about Jesus and then sending them away to sleep outside in the cold. Most of the time, our supper table was quite noisy with laughter and joking, or with one of us trying to get a reaction from my mom. Amid all of this, however, there would be moments of conversation about faith, and they didn't feel unnatural, forced, or coercive. Our guests would sometimes engage in the discussion and other times they would not, and it never took long for my siblings or me to interrupt the discussion with some kind of prank on our poor mother.

Several years ago I created a video curriculum on the topic of poverty by interviewing pastors, professors, authors, activists, and more. I called the series *Pov.ology*, and one of the many things I learned was how this odd dichotomy between evangelism and social action came to be. As is the case with many situations of polarization, over time one side of the spectrum overreacted to their counterparts in an attempt to correct an error, at which point they would err in a new way. In response the other side would also overreact and err in another way. Thus the divide in the church grew, resulting in this dichotomy that I found so incomprehensible.

Theologian and social activist Ron Sider said, "I'm glad it's the case that when we truly love people and help them out of their poverty that they're more open to the gospel, but I think it's wrong to use it as a kind of hook; then we're in danger of promoting 'rice Christians.'"[1] Sider was referring to a phenomenon that arose when Christian organizations went to countries experiencing famine, bringing a lot of food to feed the starving people, but required the people they served to first sit through a church service before receiving food. Those in need were grateful for the food, and many people "converted" to Christianity, which then was marked as a missionary success. However, those in need converted to Christianity only because they wanted the food. As soon as the organization left, these people returned to their former religions. This phenomenon happened repeatedly, and these temporary converts began to be referred to as "rice Christians" because their dedication to Christianity was not a matter of faith but of food. They jumped through the hoops put forward by the missionaries so they wouldn't be forced to starve. In terms of healing broken relationships, these programs did little to heal people's relationships with God, others, or themselves. They filled some empty stomachs and prevented some starvation, but this way of forcing the gospel on people was neither helpful nor biblically faithful. These missionaries were not making true disciples of all nations; they had instead stumbled on a way of getting people to publicly convert to Christianity by giving food only to those who would attend these services.

While I am a big proponent of biblical preaching, I do struggle with the model that forces people to sit through church services in which they would otherwise have no interest. There is a difference between entering someone's home and encountering the faith that their household lives by and being required to hear an entire sermon before receiving food from an agency program. When Jesus performed miracles and fed thousands, he never forced anyone to become his follower. Sure, he invited people to follow him, but at other times it seemed like Jesus was much less concerned with increasing the number of converts and much more concerned with simply being faithful to the ministry God had sent him to do. So Jesus healed the blind, the lame, and the sick. He fed people and he ate with them. And yes, there were many times when he did in fact preach. Other times he healed people, said a few words to them, and simply moved on, saying, "Rise and go; your faith has made you well" (Luke 17:19).

Some people embrace a philosophy of ministry that fails to do anything that demonstrates love and care to those in poverty. They favor ministries that are entirely spiritual in nature and neglect physical needs entirely. While this description may be a mild caricature, it does illustrate one extreme of this spectrum between living our faith with words and deeds.

What I admire about those on this end of the spectrum is their dedication to the Bible and to following the words of Jesus in the great commission, where we are instructed to "make disciples of all nations, baptizing them in the name of the Father and of the Son and of the Holy Spirit, and teaching them to obey everything I have commanded you" (Matthew 28:19-20). They have a zeal to spread the gospel, meaning the "good news" about Jesus. I admire how they are unashamed of their faith and that their ministries really do seek to help bring healing to the broken relationships between people and their Creator.

As is so often the case, where this movement goes wrong is not necessarily in what it affirms, but in what it ignores. It ignores the healing of other relationships that cause poverty. At times it ignores physical poverty altogether and focuses only on proselytizing. Since so many people live in poverty, it sometimes fails to meet people where they are. Those who are part of this movement neglect the physical world in favor of the spiritual world, focusing on heaven but ignoring the earth. What they forget is that in the incarnation, Jesus left heaven to come to earth, and that in the beginning, God made this physical world and called it "good." My friend Shannon Doerksen has written in her blog about the importance of materiality, and the idea that we were not accidentally placed in a physical world with physical realities. She writes, "We, body and mind, are God's workmanship, as is the world we live in. Christ embraced creation in his incarnation and redeemed it rather than discarding or ignoring it."[2]

Another thing that makes me uneasy about ignoring suffering, poverty, and the material world in general is how easily the church can begin to appear to be like the people in Amos 5 or Isaiah 1. These people had their religious events, their sacrifices, their readings and messages. The content of their services and rituals was done to the letter, but the way they lived in the world ignored oppression and poverty. God goes so far as to say, "I hate, I despise your religious festivals; your assemblies are a stench to me" (Amos 5:21). Their so-called faith did not take into account their responsibility to carry that faith into the material world in tangible ways that would have resulted in the rivers of justice that God desires to see.

On the other end of the spectrum we find people who care deeply about helping others in poverty, but who at times divorce their efforts from their faith. What I deeply admire about people at this end of the spectrum is their passion to make a real difference in the world, and to use their lives to better the lives of others in real and tangible ways. Here, too, the problem isn't so much about what they affirm, but about what is neglected. To use Bryant Myers's framework, they care about helping to heal the broken relationships between people and themselves, others, and their world, but sometimes ignore the need for healing in their relationship with their Creator, who made them, who loves them, and who has a plan for their lives. There is very logical thinking behind this. Jesus tells us that being a disciple of his will result in situations where others may hate Christians because of their faithfulness to Christ (Matthew 10:22). If someone wants to simply feed more mouths, they can raise more money and appeal to more donors by leaving faith behind, or at least leaving it at home. In the short term, greater measurable results can be achieved, so long as faith isn't a vital part of it. If the goal is only physical poverty reduction, it may appear that it can be done more effectively when not combined with faith. After all, aren't Christians supposed to help others? So what is wrong with this picture?

First of all, Christians are not called to make poverty reduction our *primary* goal. While it is a noble goal, and while Jesus "pays an astonishing amount of attention to wealth,"[3] the primary goal of Christians is to be disciples of Jesus. It is paradoxical to think that we can leave Jesus out of our efforts to better accomplish the mission of Jesus. This, of course, doesn't mean that we must hold our aid and development resources hostage until people hear a sermon; it simply means we should not separate our faith from our actions. We should not be ashamed of the gospel or neglect to live it out.

Another issue that arises is that of power. We may think that if we have more power, we can use that power to do more good. Henri Nouwen writes about the difficult history that the church has to contend with: faith leaders through the centuries have not been able to resist the allure of power, ignoring how Jesus "did not cling to his divine power but emptied himself and became as we are."[4] Nouwen continues, "The long painful history of the church is the history of people ever and again tempted to choose power over love, control over the cross, being a leader over being led. . . . One thing is clear to me: The temptation of power is greatest when intimacy is a threat. Much Christian leadership is exercised by people who do not know how to develop healthy, intimate relationships and have opted for power and control instead. Many Christian empire-builders have been people unable to give and receive love."[5] Pope Francis puts it this way, "Poverty for us Christians is not a sociological, philosophical, or cultural category, no. It is theological. I might say this is the first category, because our God, the Son of God, abased himself; he made himself poor to walk along the road with us. This is our poverty:

the poverty of the flesh of Christ, the poverty that brought the Son of God to us through his incarnation. A poor Church for the poor begins by reaching out to the flesh of Christ."[6] The solution to the allure of power is to remember the way of Jesus. If we are following Jesus, we will not seek more power, but rather will seek to empty ourselves for the sake of others. Surely the same accusations around inefficiency that can mire our thinking could be leveled against our Lord, yet it was Christ who saved the world. While there are times we need to band together as Christians and even as societies around a common cause, Christians must be wary of the temptation to neglect our faith for the sake of greater power in achieving our immediate goals.

So what is the gospel, the "good news" that is at the core of the Christian faith? In the words of Jesus, "For God so loved the world that he gave his one and only Son, that whoever believes in him shall not perish but have eternal life. For God did not send his Son into the world to condemn the world, but to save the world through him" (John 3:16-17). The work of Jesus, his life, death, and resurrection, can make us right with God and give us hope for eternal salvation as well as hope for healing in our relationships here on earth. The beauty of the gospel is that for all our striving and working to be better people, we do not have to earn our salvation; in fact, we cannot earn it. It is a gift given freely. It is not a gift that can be wrapped up and handed to someone; it is the gift of belonging that wraps itself around us. This is not belonging in the way an enslaved person "belongs" to a slave owner but belonging in the way that a child belongs to their loving parent or a parent to their child. It is the gift of becoming children of God (John 1:12-13). This gospel makes us part of the family of God, and invites us to serve our new brothers and sisters, as well as to serve others while bearing witness to the message that this belonging that we experience in the family of God is not exclusive but freely available to all who would come to the cross.

A few verses in Ephesians explain this well: "For it is by grace you have been saved, through faith—and this is not from yourselves, it is the gift of God—not by works, so that no one can boast. For we are God's handiwork, created in Christ Jesus to do good works, which God prepared in advance for us to do" (Ephesians 2:8-10). Sometimes I hear people focus on the first part of this passage, which reminds us of the free gift of salvation, given not because of anything we did or could ever do to earn it. Other times I hear people talk about doing good works in the latter part of this passage, ignoring the first part. It is the love of God that draws us and enables us to belong to the divine family, and it is the love of God that sends us out to serve. Salvation isn't a matter of either love or works, grace or good deeds. It is receiving the love of God, and then expressing that love through our lives to others. Pope Francis writes, "St. Paul says that 'the love of Christ compels us,' but this 'compels us' can also be translated as 'possesses us.' And so it is: love attracts us and sends us; it draws us in and gives us to others. This tension marks the beating of the heart of the Christian."[7]

Theology professor Patrick Franklin writes about an understanding of the church that transcends this oversimplified false dichotomy. According to Franklin, we can be a church that emphasizes God's love and the way that people ought to worship—you know, the usual churchy things. He also believes that this doesn't preclude or prevent the church from doing the other things it is called to do. He believes that we can properly understand the church "both as a community of love and worship and as an agent of social justice that stands in solidarity with 'the least of these'—the poor, hungry, sick, rejected, oppressed, and suffering other."[8]

Ron Sider has said, "Fortunately in my lifetime we have seen evangelical Christians move from only being concerned with evangelism to being concerned with both evangelism and social action. . . . More and more evangelicals all around the world are doing both."[9] I am thankful for this growing trend, and hope that more people can see these two concerns not as competing versions of the gospel, but as different parts of the same and only gospel.[10] The gospel is truly good news for the world. While it gives us a living hope for eternity, it also empowers us to find healing and to live as God's people here on earth.

Recently, I was visiting with my friend Elaine, who is a missionary together with her husband Bruce. As we were talking one morning around our breakfast table, she put it this way, "I believe you can do social good without proclaiming the gospel, but I don't believe you can share the gospel without also doing social good." The gospel prepares us for eternity, but it is an eternity that begins each day as we seek that God's will be done "on earth as it is in heaven" (Matthew 6:10). We must embrace the primacy of Jesus and the good news that we are sent to proclaim, not only by speaking it with our lips, but also by demonstrating it with our lives and actions.

Catherine and William Booth, the founders of the Salvation Army, believed both in sharing the gospel and in helping others. William is quoted as saying, "It is impossible to comfort men's hearts with the love of God when their feet are perishing with cold."[11] Yet this same man also said, "To get a man soundly saved it is not enough to put on him a pair of new breeches, to give him regular work, or even to give him a University education. These things are all outside a man, and if the inside remains unchanged you have wasted your labor. You must in some way or other graft upon the man's nature a new nature, which has in it the element of the Divine."[12] While many of us might view these two truths as existing in tension with each other, the Booths and the Salvation Army exemplify how these truths need not be in tension with each other, but rather function like two hands of the same person working together for the glory of God.

In theory all of this sounds fairly simple and straightforward: be willing to share the good news about Jesus, and also work for the good of those on the margins in our community as an expression of the gospel. Yet what happens when the gospel doesn't start out in a neutral place? In Canada, Christianity carries a lot of baggage among Indigenous communities. For many years, churches helped perpetuate abuses among Indigenous peoples through the residential school program, not to mention the disgraceful legacy of the Doctrine of Discovery that continues to impact our Indigenous neighbors today. Kyle Mason is the founder of an urban ministry that used to operate in Winnipeg's North End, and he talks about the tensions that were present in such situations:

> We operate in a neighborhood that is largely Indigenous, and history, the Canadian government, and Christianity have not been kind to we Indigenous people. A lot of evil, a lot of wrong, has happened to us in the name of the church. So if we were to say, "Hi, we're Christians," we are automatically asking people to put up walls and put up their defenses because in this neighborhood, because of all the harm that has been done in the past, the gospel is not starting at a neutral state. It is starting with a lot of knocks against it. We find that if we've built that relationship and we've built that foundation and built that respect, then we are able to show people in a very real way the real message of Jesus—the love, hope and grace. And we're not building these relationships with a secret motive to convert them. I'm getting to know this person and build this connection because they are my relative, they are my relation—Jesus loves them as much as Jesus loves me. I get the privilege of getting to know them.

Just that alone is amazing and that is valuable. But because Jesus is important in my life, that tends to spill out in my friendships and in my relationships and in my connections.[13]

When we live and work in communities where the church has failed to live as it should and thus has damaged others, it is especially important to be humble and sensitive in how we share the good news of Jesus. One could arrogantly rush into such a community, preach a sermon on a street corner, and conclude that they have done their duty. To use a farming analogy, if the ground is hard, then there will be minimal success in planting seeds unless the ground is cultivated first. Far too many people have experienced a perverted version of the gospel that espoused fear instead of friendship, control instead of communion. In such cases, sharing the gospel will look very different from what it would in places where there is a preexisting receptivity and respect for Christianity.

I am not sure where you find yourself, or what the dynamics are in your community. Regardless, there will be people from all kinds of backgrounds and all manner of dispositions toward the gospel. The way you go about sharing the gospel will be as unique as the person who is in front of you. Yet with all of this incalculable diversity, I am convinced that our lives should be ordered around the gospel of our Lord Jesus, which should influence our actions and season our speech. Don't love people just to try to convert them, but love them unconditionally as Jesus does—just as Jesus loves you. When you live out the gospel in all its simplicity and splendor, you will begin to see the image of God and the face of Christ in those around you, and they just might be able to see the same in you.

SEVEN

Get Off Your High Horse

HAVE YOU EVER HEARD OF the NGO worker named Barbie Savior? She works somewhere in Africa—though she doesn't mention the country—and she takes a lot of selfies and has a very stylish Instagram account.[1] If you haven't heard of her, there is no need to worry, because she isn't a real person. Her Instagram account is real enough, but she is a persona created by two anonymous development workers who came to see that some of their zeal for helping others was misguided and was rooted in something that is sometimes referred to as a "white savior complex."[2] The satirical account is designed to expose the patronizing and arrogant perspectives that can be prevalent in poverty reduction work. The account owners take pictures of stylish Barbie dolls posed in stereotypical ways and include captions that we can only hope are caricatures and exaggerations; captions that help expose destructive attitudes toward those in poverty.

In one post, Barbie is posed in front of a mud hut with a candy heart in her hands that says "You Are Saved," and the caption reads, in part, "I spent my Valentine's Day doing my part to end world hunger AND teaching the villagers to read . . . one candy heart at a time! #iwillbeyoursaviorbaby."[3] What is obvious in this post is that Barbie Savior thinks that she is there to save the people around her through her efforts, and that without her, these people would be hopelessly lost. Before we explore this topic further, let me put this as bluntly as I can: many of us need to get off our high horse, stop looking down on everyone else, and treat people with dignity and respect, not as some project to be fixed or some pet to entertain us. We need to stop viewing poverty-ridden communities as tourist destinations that satisfy our own emotional need to feel useful. This kind of attitude curtails the mutuality and dignity that should be central to all poverty reduction efforts. I am not against helping others, as you will have gathered by now if you are still reading this book, but attitudes like this are in desperate need of adjustment, and reveal a serious problem that runs deep. While a lot of excellent work is being done in the scholarly world around missiology and anthropology, this doesn't always filter down to the popular level, so these problems continue to plague many efforts that are intended to help others.

The problem of missionaries embracing a god complex is so common that a group of people, mostly from Uganda, started an awareness website called No White Saviors. This group of people witnessed firsthand the devastating attitudes of superiority and the negative impact of god complexes from missionaries who have come to their country. While they encourage and applaud the impulse to help others, they have witnessed the damage that this kind of pride can do. They write, "We are here to ask that if you come to help, if you say you truly love Uganda and its people, that you start listening before speaking, learning before acting and partnering instead of leading."[4] One might think that this is common sense, yet the unfortunate reality is that it is anything but common.

From time to time I enjoy going on hiking trips, spending a few days in the backcountry, enjoying God's good earth. On one such trip, my friend Abe and I were hiking in Bruce Peninsula National Park, and as often happens, we encountered a couple of other hikers. As we hiked together, I discovered that one of the men happened to work for the United Nations, in their peace building division. I became quite curious about his work and peppered him with questions—thankfully he seemed happy to talk about his work instead of being annoyed. When I asked what the process looked like and how they approach incredibly difficult situations, he repeatedly emphasized the importance of humility. There are times when workers will enter into these countries thinking they have all the answers for large and complex problems—he said this is often the case with younger, less experienced individuals. The people they are trying to help will often be polite and patiently tolerate this approach because they are in need of the resources that such a worker can provide, knowing that this is just one more person who is coming through and will eventually leave. There have been aid workers like them before, and there will be more after them. The people tolerate the ignorance and misguided zeal so that they can receive the aid that they desire. When the UN is able to help effect lasting change, however, it is often because the workers came to these regions not with all the answers, but with questions and with a desire to learn from the local people, empowering them to create a better life for themselves through solutions of which they can honestly take ownership. I believe that the humility that this UN worker told me about is desperately needed regardless of whether we are working on the scale of an international crisis or with our next-door neighbor.

Whether a short-term trip overseas to serve in some way or the work of long-term development, these kinds of self-righteous attitudes are far too common, even though they are often much more subtle than the Instagram account of Barbie Savior or arrogant UN workers. Professor Ray Vander Zaag talks about the "God complex of the rich" and, inversely, the "marred identity complex of the poor," a concept that Bryant Myers also discusses in *Walking with the Poor* (I mentioned it earlier in chapter 5). At the root of these attitudes seems to be the malformation of identity. "The poor have often internalized their poverty," says Vander Zaag. "For whatever reason, they think that they are not worthy, or capable, or deserving."[5] The inverse also happens, when those with greater material resources internalize their wealth, and come to believe that because they are financially successful, they have the answers for others about how to become as financially successful as they are. This line of thinking isn't entirely illogical, but it is detrimental. We see disparities in the world, where some people experience greater physical poverty than others and some people experience greater material and financial wealth than others, and we conclude that if we want to become like those who are wealthy and not like those in poverty, we should imitate the wealthy. This does make sense in many ways; if I wanted to learn how to be a mechanic, I wouldn't take lessons from someone who doesn't know a radiator from a muffler. This is the logic that television shows like *Shark Tank*—or the Canadian version, *Dragon's Den*—are built on. Contestants want the help of wealthy investors, pitching ideas to them and hoping to become one of the lucky few who will get an investment and an experienced ally to make their endeavor a success. While some ventures in poverty reduction can and should make use of the experts in a given field, this shift in identity is devastating to all involved. When people internalize their socioeconomic status as a foundational part of their identity, then the identity of the rich and the identity of the poor have no shared common ground, unless the poor become like the rich, or vice versa. This question of identity is no small matter as we talk about serving others and poverty reduction work.

From the perspective of the Bible, the basis and foundation for all human identity is that we are made in the image of God, and it is in this truth that rich and poor alike can come to experience one another not as *other*, but as fellow image bearers of our Creator. When we deviate from this as our foundational identity, our identities become distorted and marred. Myers writes, "There is a much deeper irony here. The non-poor suffer from the same kind of poverty as the poor. They too suffer from marred identity, but with a marring of a different kind. When the non-poor play god in the lives of other people, they have stopped being who they truly are and are assuming the role of God."[6]

When seeking to reduce poverty, one of the goals is the healing of the broken relationships between people and themselves. For people in poverty, this often involves helping them see that their poverty does not define their value or worth. Vander Zaag says, "That is what the gospel says to us . . . despite anything you could have done, God loves you. So when serving the poor, we are in a sense being Jesus in a little way that says, 'regardless of all that, you are capable and you can change your life, and you deserve to have enough to eat, healthy relationships, et cetera.' When it comes to poverty in a certain sense it is changing people's sense about themselves." He also acknowledges that this "is the hardest thing to change."[7] I believe it is equally hard—but equally important—to change the god complex that plagues so much poverty reduction work.

One added layer of difficulty in all of this is how these harmful attitudes around identity reinforce each other. Those with a god complex rush in, believing their wealth is evidence that they are suited to help others. Those in need of help who have internalized their poverty think so little of themselves that they do not resist this arrogance but view it as evidence that these other people should be leading things. They wish they could be like these new leaders while also believing themselves not worthy of such a life. They accept these new people as the source of their help, reinforcing the belief of the wealthy persons that *they* are the solution to the problem, which in turn reinforces the beliefs of those in poverty that they cannot solve *their own* problems and are not capable of helping themselves, much less capable of helping someone else. Oh, that we would break free from this dreadful cycle and instead come to see in one another people who are at once broken and also worthy of dignity and respect!

Henri Nouwen was a professor at Harvard before he left this career and began serving as a priest in one of the L'Arche communities in Toronto for people living with mental disabilities. He continued to travel as a guest speaker at various events, and he writes of how he invited one of the community members, Bill, to a speaking engagement in Washington, D.C. Before the event, Nouwen told Bill that they would be going together to serve God. So Bill often talked about the trip, wanting reassurance that they would in fact be working together. As Nouwen recounts, "He accepted as an invitation to join me in my ministry. 'We are doing this together,' he said at different times in the days before we left. 'Yes,' I kept saying, 'we are doing this together. You and I are going to Washington to proclaim the Gospel.' Bill did not for a moment doubt the truth of this."[8] During Nouwen's speech, Bill—who struggled with expressing himself verbally—came up on the stage while Nouwen was speaking. Since this was unplanned, Nouwen did not know what to do, so he kept speaking. As Nouwen would finish with one of his pages of notes, Bill would gently take it from the podium and place it neatly out of Nouwen's way, and would loudly reemphasize or affirm points here and there that Nouwen made. As the speech continued, Nouwen began to feel more at ease, and it was Bill's additions to the speech that would be what people remembered long after they left. These comments in fact helped make Nouwen's points in ways that he never could have done alone. He writes about this event, "While I was quite nervous about what to say and how to say it, Bill showed great confidence in his task. And, while I was still thinking about Bill's trip with me primarily as something that would be nice for him, Bill was, from the beginning, convinced that he was going to help me. I later came to realize that he knew better than I." [9] How often do we judge others because of the difficulties we see in their lives instead of embracing them because of our shared humanity, and learning that they, oftentimes, do in fact know better than we do? How humbling to realize how wrong he was, and how humbling to realize how wrong we so often are as well.

Some of us may struggle with the god complex that Myers and Vander Zaag talk about. This attitude is deceptively easy to develop. As a pastor I am given a literal platform every week, where people gather each Sunday to hear me speak. Of course, they don't come to hear me speak. They come to worship God, and to hear a message from the Bible. But since I am the one who often speaks that message, it is very easy to turn something good and beautiful into something about *me*. When this happens, it is not beautiful, but exposes the ugliness of pride—while both my wife and my mother would tell you that I appear quite handsome, if they were honest they both could attest to the ugliness of my pride that can lurk within. I also have many colleagues in the "helping professions" who can attest to the ease of slipping into these prideful and arrogant mentalities.

Others of us may struggle with the kind of marred identity that comes from poverty and a lack of material wealth. Even in the Global North, where poverty is not nearly as severe as in the Global South, this kind of attitude is incredibly easy to develop. I have known several people, myself included, who dreamed of going to college but struggled to believe they belonged there. They grew up in a small town in relatively poor families and didn't believe that they were worthy or good enough to do it.

They would make comments about being simple "country folk" and would imply that they didn't belong in the ivory towers of academia. They believed that their lack of material wealth meant that they would not be as smart as their wealthy, urban classmates. Then, for those who did end up starting their studies, they almost quit several times as they progressed, feeling that they didn't fit in and feeling inferior to their classmates. This kind of marred identity complex has a huge impact on those who live with it. From my past, what amazes me now is how easy it would have been for me to sabotage my own education before I even had a chance to start, because of this broken relationship with myself. Had it not been for my wife's influence, I likely would have quit, which would have drastically changed the direction of my life and career. It also amazes me how this mentality sometimes comes up again in my life, seemingly out of nowhere, in ways that make life a lot more difficult

It is possible for people like me to experience both of these false beliefs about ourselves. Perhaps you grew up in poverty but no longer experience it, or at least not as acutely. Or perhaps, as the middle class continues to erode, you are part of the masses of people who have moved into a lower socioeconomic bracket. The good news is that no matter which problem of identity we struggle with, the solution for all of them is to return to the truth about who we are, according to the one who made us. First, we remember that we are all made in the image of God, regardless of the circumstance we find ourselves in, and second, we must come back to the gospel that reminds us that while all have sinned, through Jesus all can receive grace, forgiveness, and healing as we become part of God's family (Romans 3:23-30).

The apostle Paul gives this instruction, "Do not think of yourself more highly than you ought, but rather think of yourself with sober judgment" (Romans 12:3). He goes on to say that each person has been given a gift that is to be used to serve others. Whether we are plagued with an inflated view of our own importance or with a perspective that devalues our own worth and ability, a reminder to think soberly is much needed in today's world. Just as alcohol distorts one's judgment, so too do these faulty foundations for our identities distort our view of ourselves and the roles we play. To think soberly is to invite ourselves to remove these distortions and view ourselves from the perspective of God. Paul invites his readers to consider what gifts they do in fact have to offer, and to use them to serve faithfully, in whatever capacity that may be. This means that for some, they should step back from trying to save the world and simply fulfill their own role, recognizing it as one function in the vast body of Christ. For others this means recognizing that they do indeed have something to offer, and that they have been created by God to fulfill a purpose in this life.

For all the challenges that my family faced growing up, I am thankful that my parents didn't buy into the lie that they had nothing to offer, and while it may have been just a bowl of soup and a night on our couch, over the years they helped countless people and made a tangible difference to many. While this didn't protect me entirely from thinking less of myself because of our lack of worldly goods, it did help me see in tangible ways the large influence that people can have even if they are unable to write large checks to charity. I believe one of our world's most underappreciated resources is the efforts and gifts of those around the world who live in poverty; and that more than that, they are the world's most underappreciated people. We would do well to learn how to receive the incredible gifts that these dear friends have to offer.

EIGHT

Learning to Receive

THE FAMILIAR DING RANG OUT from my computer notifying me of a new email. I went to check it and discovered an email money transfer, sent at an unexpected time from a very unexpected source. The sender's name was Shelley, a single mother from our congregation who worked three jobs in order to take care of her son. She was always busy, always juggling her work schedules, and desperately trying to spend time with her child while also providing for him financially. It wasn't easy to do both, and now she was sending me money that she said was specifically for me, not the church.

Shelley was sending us this generous gift because our family had gone through "a series of unfortunate events" that indeed seemed like it was out of a Lemony Snicket novel. During 2018, I had serious medical struggles, suffering forty seizures over the course of five months. This meant countless specialist appointments and expensive medications, not to mention the pain and uncertainty that accompanied such a dramatic medical issue. My driver's license was suspended, so my wife also needed to take time off work to drive me to and from these appointments in neighboring cities. During this time, our town had a major flood, which affected our home and caused tens of thousands of dollars in damage. We lost many of our belongings, including most of our children's toys. To top things off, our four-year-old son was scheduled to have surgery to remove his tonsils and adenoids. While I continued pastoring during this time, there was much uncertainty about my ability to continue. Had things gotten any worse, I would have had to resign from my position and apply for social assistance, or to use the more common but pejorative term, welfare. I know well the prejudice against people on welfare. Not only were doctors and social workers talking to me about the possibility of needing to stop working, but my denominational leaders were also having conversations with me and our church leadership about planning for this possibility. It was all very heavy, like a bad dream come to life.

We were struggling. They say that we can taste a bit of heaven on earth, but during this season I thought that I had a small taste of hell. Yet it was during all of this that Shelley gave us a financial gift. It didn't solve all our problems, but it sure did help at a time when we needed it. We had countless gifts of food, time, and childcare from our congregation, but other than one anonymous contribution in the mail (thanks, whoever you are!), Shelley was the only person who helped by offering us a financial gift. And she did it more than once.

I must admit that I had a hard time accepting it. This was a person whom our congregation had aided several times financially in emergency situations. It felt somehow backward to accept help from her. The more I examined my hesitation, however, the more it became clear that its source could be summed up in one word: pride. There, I said it, pride—such a nasty little word, a sin of which I was indeed guilty. I'm a pastor after all, and my entire profession is largely geared around helping others. I am supposed to be the strong one, the one who has it all together. But I didn't have it all together, and if I was honest, we really needed that kind of help. That incredible need was a large part of my reason for accepting it, even though doing so was a bit uncomfortable for me. This act of accepting a gift—from someone in need herself—taught me more than I ever could have imagined.

I knew rejecting the gift would be rude and disrespectful. I knew that Shelley felt that the Lord had asked her to make this sacrifice for us, and that in order for her to be obedient to what she felt God was asking her to do, she needed to give it. While her gift was an outflowing of love and care for us, it was also an outflowing of her love and care for God. She was, and is, our dear friend, and she helped us out as we had helped her in the past. Proverbs 17:17 says, "A friend is always loyal, and a brother is born to help in time of need" (NLT). Shelley was taking her call to be our spiritual family seriously, and had I refused her gift, I would have robbed her of the blessing of giving, and rejected the very relationship that connected us in the first place. Shelley was being a spiritual sister to us and wanted to help because that is simply what family does, even though the only blood that connects us is the blood of Jesus.

* * *

It turns out that having difficulty receiving from others is a remarkably common but devastating problem. One psychotherapist I know shared that this is an issue that many of his patients deal with, and that it is evidence of one's own brokenness, which often leads to many other broken relationships.

When my wife and I were engaged, we attended a conference as part of our preparation for marriage. On the way, we had to drive through Calgary, and we got hopelessly lost. At that time, GPS devices had been invented but were quite expensive, so we were relying on maps to get us there. We began bickering, which led to arguing, which led to more heated arguing, and eventually an icy silence on my part. This infuriated my lovely bride-to-be and we eventually arrived at this conference about marriage thoroughly miffed with one another. We carried our belongings to our separate hotel rooms in the conference center, and after a few minutes she came to see if I was ready to go to the first session.

Our dispute continued until Emily broke through the point-less back and forth and said she thought I was a beautiful person. I suddenly became irrationally furious. I told her to never say that again. I yelled those words at her, and then broke down in tears. It took us awhile to get to the bottom of my anger, but in that moment, I believed I was not worthy of love and that our whole relationship would soon fall apart if she really knew me. I knew how to handle criticism, insults, and direct attacks, but not compliments. Not love. We worked through it, and thankfully we weren't even late for the first session of the conference. And after that, we purchased our first GPS.

This little episode showed me in stark terms how my inability to accept the love of my bride-to-be was immensely destructive to this life-giving relationship. The ability to receive from others is essential to any real and meaningful relationship. Imagine my surprise all these years later when I realized that the lesson I had learned in my marriage was now so hard to relearn as a pastor. Healthy relationships cannot exist in the absence of a willing-ness to *both* give and receive.

* * *

I have come to love the word *mutuality*. This word implies co-operation, mutual respect, and an acknowledgment of a shared dignity and common purpose. As we think about poverty, we should take time to ponder what kinds of relationships we have with those whom we seek to serve. Are they one-sided? Are we viewing ourselves as the ones with all the answers or all the re-sources and viewing others as helpless victims? Of course, there are times when tragedy strikes and people are truly helpless *in that moment*. When the floodwaters come, who is powerful enough to make them stop? Yet even then, there is a difference between offering emergency support in a time of crisis and an ongoing one-sided relationship.

In *When Helping Hurts*, a helpful distinction is made be-tween emergency aid and development. When disaster strikes, such as a hurricane or tsunami, long-term development issues are largely ignored for the moment, as there is simply a need for emergency medical attention and basic necessities like food, shelter, and clothing, and thus aid organizations rush in as fast as they can. When it comes to long-term development, however, there is a helpful rule of thumb: "Do not do things for people that they can do for themselves."[1] The basic concept of this rule is that doing things for people when they are perfectly capa-ble of doing them for themselves is patronizing. Not following this rule has resulted in untold amounts of damage all over the world. This is a very useful general principle, even though there are definite exceptions.

In my tight-knit church community, one way that love and care are expressed is through food. This is such a strong cultural element of the various Mennonite communities I have known that I have come to suspect that it is our "love language." For Emily and me, the births of our children were relatively easy ones, and in the weeks afterward we were still capable of mak-ing food for ourselves, but it certainly was nice when someone brought us a casserole. When one of the men in our community had a knee replacement surgery, his wife was also still capable of cooking, but we arranged for people to bring food. Why? Because we love each other and want to show that care in a tan-gible way. While everyone has at one time or another been the recipient of such hospitality, everyone is also expected to participate as they are able and as needs arise. There is a give-and-take, there is the blessing of giving and the blessing of receiving. It isn't done in a way that makes the recipient feel inadequate or undignified. It is simply a spiritual family showing love to one another. If you do something for others that they *can* do for themselves, just be sure that it is done in the context of mutuality and not in a way that makes them feel inferior.

When there is an unwillingness to receive, relationships break down. This kind of pride can even destroy relationships that were once very close. Think of Bryant Myers's definition of poverty: a series of broken relationships. We cannot have a proper relationship with someone if we only give to them and never receive. That isn't much of a relationship at all. While giving to others shows them that we care enough to sacrifice something for their sake, it is in receiving from others that we demonstrate that they are more than a project and that they have something of value to offer this world as well. While in giving we participate in the mission of God for the benefit of others, it is in receiving that others take part in the mission of God for the benefit of us— and in all things, whether giving or receiving, we can together work for the glory of God.

When we consider the very purpose of the church, we can also begin to see things more clearly. Professor Patrick Franklin writes that "the Christian Church community exists *both* as an end in itself *and* as a means to a greater end."[2] What he is getting at is that part of the mission of God is to sustain the church, "a community of love and new life, in which people live in restored communion with God and one another."[3] He writes further about how the church also exists for the sake of others, in keeping with the example of Jesus. He understands the church both as "a community of love and worship and as an agent of social justice."[4] This helps us see the greater importance in receiving;

for we too are necessary recipients of care in God's mission to the world.

While it is a bit easier to understand the concept of receiving and mutuality on the level of our interpersonal relationships, we may wonder how this might play out on a larger scale in terms of international development work. Note that the receiving that I am talking about is not just money or food, but also ideas, direction, and wisdom—among other things.

After graduating from high school, I didn't have many friends my own age who stuck around the small Alberta town where I lived. As a result, most of the friends I spent time with were middle-aged or older. One man named Gordy was an empty-nester whom I knew through a prayer meeting we both attended every Wednesday. He and his wife decided to go overseas to serve aboard a cruise ship that had been converted into a traveling hospital. I greatly admired his boldness to move so far away at that stage of life, and to offer his time and effort to such a noble endeavor. Gordy and his wife fulfilled their term, and eventually returned to our small town. I was full of questions for him, and I loved listening to his stories. As we enjoyed our coffee—Gordy always brought his own cream because ours was too light for his taste—I felt like a sponge, soaking up all his stories of service, sacrifice, and struggle.

One day Gordy told me a story about some missionaries who came to a community armed with financial resources, human resources, and construction know-how. These missionaries offered to build the town a hospital, a school, or something of the sort. The community leaders deliberated, and then made the humble request that the missionaries build a soccer field. The missionaries shook their heads, condescendingly thinking that they knew what was best. Well, it turns out hospitals and schools had been built before and never lasted long. The community was deeply divided, and there wasn't enough unity for them to sustain such initiatives despite being given a building. The missionaries initially rejected the idea, but eventually gave in and built the community a soccer field, not really knowing why it was requested. The soccer field brought people together, and as they began to encounter one another in this way, their relationships were healed and restored. Not long after, they were able to build and sustain a hospital and school on their own.

While this is a beautiful story, it is also a painful one for those of us seeking to help others because it reminds us of how often we assume we know better than the people we are trying to serve. We assume that because we are not the ones in material poverty, we must know what others' needs are or how to solve their problems. Most of us don't know as much as we would like to think. When people learn to listen to one another and view others as people, and not as projects, transformation begins in profound ways. These missionaries completely underestimated the capacity and wisdom of the local leaders, and they completely missed noticing the truest need. It wasn't for a hospital or school, but for the community members to be able to encounter one another in ways that could heal their broken relationships and restore the unity within their community. The elders knew this well, and they were incredibly wise to insist on what they did. While the missionaries were a bit slow to come on board with the idea, they eventually did, making this a story of people learning to serve others with mutuality and respect. While those seeking to help materially may have a lot of physical and financial resources, those we serve often have just as much or more to offer their own communities that may not be as easy to quantify as money, but is priceless nonetheless.

Ray Vander Zaag, who teaches international development, put it this way:

If you're not in relationship with someone, then it's really hard to help them. Sometimes that relationship can be through denominational agencies and can be a bit more remote, but if you don't have some sense of connection and that there is a two-way thing going on, then it's really hard to help. The best example of that is the street person you walk by; you're not in a relationship with them, and you can throw a toonie[5] in their cup, but you have no clue what that toonie is actually going to do for them—and it's really hard to be in relationship with them, because then you would have to stop and maybe take them for a coffee. Even then, their problems might be really long term, and if you were really serious about helping that person you would have to make a long-term commitment. That, for me, is the hard part about helping people, especially those who are far away, because of that relationship piece.[6]

The importance of receiving and the concept of mutuality, dignity, and respect in relationships isn't just some popular modern idea. There is much in the Bible that pushes us to think in this way. When we examine the work of God in the Bible, we find that the good Lord does in fact treat us with a great deal of mutuality and dignity.

One of the first examples we see in the Bible is that humanity was made as caretakers and stewards of the wonderful world that God created. While God created the earth, it was made with the specific intention that God would work alongside humanity to care for it. All of this was the case before sin even entered the world.

Later we see in the book of 1 Samuel that the people demanded a king over their nation, and while God warned them of the consequences of this choice, the Lord did not stand in the way of their choice but allowed Israel to be co-creators of their own reality. God showed them respect and dignity by allowing them to have a say about their own future.

Consider the entire concept of what we call "the gospel." It is in the gospel that we learn we can live in right relationship with God through the work of Jesus, something that is not forced upon us, but offered freely. We then have a choice to enter this relationship with God, or to reject it. There is no coercion or manipulation, just a choice given to us, the *imago Dei*, the creatures made in the very image of God. We are given full authority for our own decision about this, though the gift we are offered is not something we could ever obtain on our own.

A peculiar story recorded in John 13 is that of Jesus washing the feet of his disciples. This was a task typically given to servants. After all, feet get pretty dirty when walking in sandals through dusty terrain. Yet Jesus, the teacher and honored leader of this motley band of disciples, takes the position of a humble servant. Jesus is reversing the cultural script and serves his disciples, instead of being served. This would have felt incredibly unnatural or uncomfortable for them.

When Jesus gets to Peter, Peter refuses to allow Jesus to wash his feet. Jesus responds by saying, "Unless I wash you, you have no part with me" (John 13:8). Peter was having a hard time receiving. He was the disciple. He was the one to serve Jesus. Allowing Jesus to serve him was backward—it wasn't how things were supposed to be. Then Jesus shatters that kind of thinking: Peter could not be Jesus' disciple unless he first received what Jesus was there to give him.

This is one of the profound truths of the gospel, that we are able to receive salvation from Jesus, who serves us and washes us clean from all sin and unrighteousness. The very basis of receiving salvation involves learning how to receive. So how have we become so twisted around to think that we always must be the ones to give, and never the ones to receive? We, like Peter, are in need of the work of Jesus. And while nobody can take the place of Jesus, the church is referred to in the New Testament as the body of Christ. The church is the hands and feet of Jesus doing his work in the world. In this story of Jesus washing the feet of the disciples, we see that Jesus is setting an example for us as people who ought to serve others. Jesus also gives direct instruction that in order to belong to Christ, we must also be willing to receive his ministry to us.

Could it be that in all our busy work and insistence that we are the ones who should be serving, some of us have come to have no part in Christ because we are unwilling to receive from him through his body? Is it possible that for all our good intentions, we have become like Peter and instinctively refuse the gifts of Christ? In remembering Jesus' example of serving others, have we forgotten that in order to belong to Christ we also must receive from him? Maybe we think it makes us look weak, or maybe it brings us face-to-face with needs in ourselves that we would rather ignore. Perhaps it shatters our illusions of complete self-sufficiency or dismantles our god complex. Yet these notions are so far from what the gospel teaches. We need Jesus, and as much as we need him, we also need others to serve us as the body of Christ in tangible and practical ways. We need Jesus to work in our lives through others just as much as they need the work of God through us.

I am *not* saying that refusing a gift from someone means that one's salvation is in jeopardy. Let me explain. Christians believe that part of our responsibility as disciples of Jesus is to be more like him. Since Jesus showed love to others, helping meet their needs in many ways, we ought to do the same. This example was given clearly by Jesus and lived out in the early church. We believe that God works through people, and when we serve others we take part in the very mission of God. In the same line of thinking, it stands to reason that if this is God's mission, and God is using people to accomplish his purposes, then other people will also be involved in the process. It then means that we will not simply be giving all the time, but also receiving. We will not be the ones in control and in charge of what happens, but we will, together with others, seek to accomplish the work of God in a way that is life-giving to all parties involved—fostering healthy relationships in the process. What I am suggesting is that if, like Peter, we only do what we want to do and do not accept the ministry of Christ himself, then we may end up doing a lot of things that look good on the outside but that have no part in Jesus.

If there is hope for healing the broken relationships at the root of poverty, then we must realize that an unwillingness to receive from others is one way that many relationships are broken. This receiving may come in the form of money, time, acts of service, advice, wisdom, and more. In learning to properly receive, we recognize that the work we do for God isn't just about us. It is the very work of Jesus. When we refuse to receive, we might be scorning something that God wishes us to have. In times of receiving advice or wisdom, Proverbs puts it nicely: "The way of fools seems right to them, but the wise listen to advice" (Proverbs 12:15). Wisdom is also an important thing to learn to receive, as my friend Gordy taught me through his excellent anecdotes. In learning to receive, we come to realize that serving Jesus by serving others is about so much more than our own personal faith. It reminds us that God loves and values others, and desires to partner with them as well to accomplish God's purpose in this world.

* * *

In our little congregation, on quite a few occasions we have spent money and time helping our single mothers, who as the sole providers for themselves and their children have often struggled financially. Yet as a congregation, while we have pooled money and resources to help meet their basic needs, it would be a huge mistake to act as if our single mothers are helpless or somehow substandard Christians. Between the various single mothers in our congregation, they have run our Sunday school program, started and continue to run our women's prayer meeting, and begun chapel services in the community for people with disabilities. They are involved in kids' Bible clubs and they are the ones who had a vision for what would eventually become our church's youth program. If that wasn't enough, they have helped spearhead fundraisers for many other people in need within our community.

To give you some perspective, there are only three of them. This small number makes this list of accomplishments all the more impressive. Sure, our church has spent some money on our single moms. Yet I shudder to think of the spiritual loss to our church and community if we were without them. They are some of our movers and shakers, and I wouldn't ever dare to call them "helpless." They, along with the rest of our congregation, have taught me the power of mutuality in such relationships. While they don't have much by way of worldly goods or money or typical forms of power, they are a force to be reckoned with in the kingdom of God. They taught me and are teaching me that one does not need to be rich to do the work of Jesus.

If we are going to participate in the mission of God as it pertains to reducing various forms of poverty, then we must be willing to receive the resources and partners that God gives us to do this work. This means that we must recognize our own deficiencies and remember that we don't know it all, we can't do it all, and we don't have it all. We must be willing to receive from God through others in order to accomplish this task. It is simply too big for any one person or organization to do on their own; we need God and we need one another. If we are not willing to receive from God through others, then we must question whether the work we are doing is even the work of God to begin with.

NINE

Mental Illness, Addictions, and Self-Care

PATTY LOVED HER SISTER JUNE. Patty believed that they had a wonderful childhood together, but as they entered the teenage years, Patty discovered that June had been abused for years by a family friend. June began to sink into a deep depression, but wouldn't let Patty tell anyone what had happened. June's depression got worse, and then she started to have panic attacks. June struggled in school, and fell in with "the wrong crowd," and she began using drugs to cope with her trauma. Over time, her addictions became frightful, leading June to steal from her family, and eventually even physically assault Patty in a search for her next fix. Patty kept trying to help her sister, and while sometimes it would appear that June was making progress, June would just take advantage of Patty's generosity. As the years went by, Patty eventually got married and had children, but she still longed to help her sister. Patty blamed herself for June's problems because she never spoke up about the abuses of June's childhood. After not having seen her sister for a couple of years, one day when Patty was walking down a street she saw her sister camped out in a little cardboard dwelling in a back alley. When Patty had lived on her own she wouldn't have hesitated to try to bring her sister back home, even if it meant that June would steal from her and run away in the middle of the night, or that if June couldn't find anything to take, she might threaten to hurt Patty in order to somehow get money. Now that Patty had children at home, she didn't know what to do. She still blamed herself and carried a lot of guilt, but now she also had children to care for. In the past she had risked her own safety, but could she, or should she, risk the safety of her children?

While the details and specifics of the above story are fictional, the issues pertaining to mental illness, addictions, boundaries, and self-care are incredibly important in the discussion of poverty. Mark Dalley works for the Salvation Army and became a friend of mine through some classes we took together. He says that in his experience, most people that have come through their programs seeking help also have to deal with some form of mental illness. Mental illness is a scourge on our society, and I suspect that most of us know someone who has struggled with it significantly. I am happy to say that even in my lifetime the stigma around mental illness seems to have lessened, but we still have a long way to go in our society before we get to a place of seeing mental illness as a health issue similar to other illnesses or diseases. Mental illness can be just as devastating as cancer or paralysis, even though it can be much harder to see or understand.

In the previous chapter I wrote about a time when I experienced forty seizures over a period of several months. They looked just like grand mal seizures, so doctors initially diagnosed me with epilepsy. When the treatments for epilepsy proved unsuccessful, I underwent significant testing, and the doctors concluded that I didn't have epilepsy, but a disorder called psychogenic non-epileptic seizures. The condition is not very well known, but it is classified as a mental illness in which the brain translates particular kinds of stress into physical symptoms, in my case causing me to lose consciousness and have a seizure. After receiving a proper diagnosis, and finding out that the powerful medications I was prescribed only worsened matters, the doctors were finally able to help me get the seizures under control. I came frightfully close to having to leave my job and ministry. This would have had devastating consequences for my family's material well-being, all because of something going on in my brain that was outside my control. While I am no expert on the subject of mental illness, I can testify to the fact that it can indiscriminately affect anyone, and that trite platitudes do little to help someone experiencing it. Mental illness can and does cause poverty, and this is something of which we should all be aware.

So what do you do in situations where mental illness has led to someone's poverty? That's the million-dollar question, for which I have no easy answer. I will, however, offer a few places to start.

The first thing you could do is to educate yourself about mental illness. In Canada and the United States a course called Mental Health First Aid seeks to equip people to help others in emergency situations, much like normal first aid teaches some basics for medical emergencies.

The second thing you could do is identify resources in your community to which you could refer someone. As a pastor, people come to me with all manner of questions, many of them completely outside my realm of knowledge and experience. I am not a mental health professional, so when someone is in need of such services, I find helpful places to refer them to where they can access those services. Do not try to be someone's therapist, as it is very possible to do more harm than good. It is better to simply be their friend, and encourage them to see someone who can actually help.

You should be aware, however, that suggesting that someone is in need of mental health services can be taken as an insult or an attack against their character. Being gentle and respectful in making such recommendations is incredibly important; however, no matter how gently you speak, when people carry entrenched stigma toward others with mental illness they will not easily acknowledge that it may be a reality in their own life. Bringing this truth to light can threaten to shatter their illusions about themselves, and they may choose to withdraw from the relationship, insisting you destroyed the friendship when all you did was seek their well-being. Others, however, may experience profound relief at such a recommendation because it gives them some form of permission to get the help they didn't allow themselves to receive before.

Third, you can work to help reduce the stigma around mental illness, and to help reduce the shame people feel about seeking help. This is something that anybody can do, simply by suspending our urge to condemn what we do not understand. If everyone in our society would do this simple thing, it would help far more people feel comfortable to seek the help they need.

Finally, it is important to simply be a friend who listens patiently and seeks to understand what others are going through. Sometimes you may feel that you need to jump into problemsolving for someone, but resist that urge, and simply listen for a while. My wife is much better at this than I am; I can be fairly quick to offer solutions or advice, but simply being present and listening to people can go a long way.

When it comes to mental illness, things can get so complicated and are often so specific to an individual's circumstances that I hesitate to write too extensively about it. But if we seek to reduce the poverty in our communities, we would be remiss to ignore mental illness and its impact in our world.

* * *

Like mental illness, addiction, sadly, is common, and people suffer from it in varying degrees. Some are able to maintain jobs, while others end up on the streets. It has devastated families and continues to cause untold harm to those who suffer from it. Addiction is so commonplace that it is often referred to as an epidemic. As with the above discussion about mental illness, I am not an expert on addiction, but will offer a few thoughts.

First, as with mental illness, finding ways to educate yourself about addictions can go a long way to helping you learn how to help someone, or even how to deal with addictions in your own life. Such education can at least help prevent you from doing more harm than good.

Second, because of the nature of addiction, it puts people into a different frame of mind, which can at times be dangerous for those around them as well. A measure of caution is warranted if someone is under the influence of a substance. My wife grew up as the daughter of missionaries who, in their mission work, would do what they could to help those living on the streets in their community. When she was about fifteen years old, she came upon two men whom she knew lived on the street and who were clearly intoxicated. They started arguing, and then started fighting violently. She tried to tell them to stop, but when that didn't work, she got in the middle and stood between the two men. Miraculously, she didn't get hurt, but her story is an example of what *not* to do. She should have called an adult trained in crisis intervention instead of getting involved herself. Neither of those men were in their right mind because of the alcohol they had consumed, which meant getting in the middle of their fight endangered her own life. When we risk our own well-being to help others, we are not only risking something for ourselves, but also risking something on behalf of other people. Our lives are not isolated from the communities to which we belong, so when someone hurts us, they also hurt those who love us or care for us. When we risk our own well-being, we are also risking pain for those around us. All that to say, if you seek to help someone dealing with addictions, be careful about how you go about it—your well-being is also important.

The reason we typically want to help someone battling addiction is because we have some kind of relationship with them. And seeking to help our friends and loved ones is a good thing. I have had numerous friends over the years whom I have tried to help leave addictions behind. One such situation was in high school. I worked at a small video rental store, and my friend would come in to chat from time to time. I knew he drank too much and did a significant amount of drugs, and I tried to encourage him to stop. On a slow night he walked into the store while I was working, and after seeing that nobody was in the store, he went on a rant about how hurt he was that Christians would judge him and tell him to simply "get off the drugs" and act in ways that were condemning. I felt so bad. I knew I had told him to get off the drugs many times. So I apologized as soon as he finished his rant. I still can't forget the look on his face. He blinked a few times, clearly confused, and said "What?" I explained how I felt bad because I knew that I had often told him to get off the drugs. He looked irritated, and said, "Kevin, you're an idiot. I'm not talking about you." He went on to talk about others in the church I went to whom he felt judged by. I knew that I told him to stop doing drugs more often than any of the other people whose names he mentioned, yet when it came from me he wasn't offended. So what was the difference? The difference was that they would say their piece and walk away, while

I would say it and then invite him to go for wings or to watch a movie. The difference was that he was my friend and he knew it. He knew that when I suggested he stop doing drugs it was because I cared for him, but when others said it, their motive was condemnation, not kindness. I would never go along with my friend to a party where there would be alcohol or drugs. I didn't want to go through the peer pressure and risk doing something I'd regret, nor did I want to experience what he was capable of when his inhibitions were gone. But I cared about my friend, and that day at the video store I found out that he really did appreciate our friendship.

In 2015 a TED Talk brought to light the importance of relationships in the world of addiction. The speaker, Johann Hari, went on a quest of sorts to learn more about addictions and how to help those in his life who struggled with them. The dominant way of thinking had previously been that there are "chemical hooks" in some substances that make the body addicted to them to the point that the body actually needs the substance to function. While this isn't entirely wrong, it painted a picture of addiction as a purely physiological phenomena, where an addicted person's body simply craves their substance of choice the way all our bodies crave food to eat and air to breathe.

This understanding is largely based on experiments conducted on rats who were put in cages and given the options of normal water and water laced with heroin or cocaine. In those initial experiments, all the rats became addicted and virtually all of them overdosed on the drugs and died. Eventually, some researchers began to question this experiment, because they believed that the environment that these rats were in surely had some impact as well. The rats were isolated, placed in cages, with nothing around them resembling their normal environment. One researcher, Bruce Alexander, did an experiment known as the "Rat Park experiment," where he created an environment that rats would enjoy, and more importantly, put a bunch of rats together.[1] In this environment, the rats almost always preferred the normal water. Hari says of the rats, "You go from almost one hundred percent overdose when they're isolated to zero percent overdose when they have happy and connected lives."[2] He ends his TED Talk with this statement, "For one hundred years now, we've been singing war songs about addicts. I think all along we should have been singing love songs to them, because the opposite of addiction is not sobriety. The opposite of addiction is connection."[3] This emerging research is changing the way people view addiction, and it is beginning to reveal the amazing power of positive relational connections.

Chris Arnade was a Wall Street banker who left that life behind, and for several years spent time in what he calls "back row America." He went to the small towns or parts of cities where poverty runs rampant—the places visitors are typically told *not* to go. He went to learn about what life was like for people living in areas known not for power or privilege but for their poverty. After years of travel, hearing countless stories from people many would avoid, he wrote a book called *Dignity: Seeking Respect in Back Row America*. Arnade is not a person of faith, but over the course of his journey he did come to have some measure of respect for religion. In the book's conclusion, he writes,

> After five years documenting addiction, poverty, and pain . . . I get asked: What are the solutions? What are the policies we should put in place? What can we do differently, beyond yell at one another? All I can say is "I don't know" or the almost equally wishy-washy "We all need to listen to each other more." It is wishy-washy, but that is what I truly believe, because our nation's problems and differences are just too big, too structural, and too deep to be solved by legislation and policy out of Washington. We need everyone—those in the back row, those in the front row—to listen to one anoth-

er and try to understand one another and understand what
they value and try to be less judgmental.[4]

Arnade has come to see the incredible importance of relationships in which people treat others with dignity.

Many who seek to make a positive difference in the world live
in a way that is sacrificial, offering their money, time, and energy to endeavors that can and do help make our world a better
place. One thing that needs to be addressed as we learn how to
think about poverty is the concept of boundaries and self-care.
Sometimes in the church we have come to glorify unnecessary
martyrdom, as if going out of our way to seek suffering and death
is a noble thing to do. There are times when people intentionally
use stories of martyrs to get people to do more for their church
or mission organization. They use those stories to try to persuade
people to give more, even to the point of burnout. Leaders use
this approach because it is remarkably effective at inspiring people to do what they want—but that doesn't make it right.

Jonathan Hollingsworth writes about his own tragic missions
experiences in *Runaway Radical: A Young Man's Reckless Journey
to Save the World*. He explains how he fell into a misguided way
of thinking that ended in a devastating burnout. As the title
suggests, he bought into the idea that it was his job to save the
world, and that he was always supposed to give more in order
to please God. He came to realize that some of the leaders he
had been serving under had used him to advance their organization, but cared little for the ways of God, or for Hollingsworth's
well-being. He writes, "When I came home, I had trouble separating the words of Jesus from the words of the manipulators
and legalists who had hurt me. And sometimes I still have trouble with that."[5] Hollingsworth, like many others, burned out
after being applauded for neglecting appropriate self-care and
ignoring healthy boundaries.

While God's strength is limitless, ours is not. We have to deal with the fact that we cannot do everything. We have to learn how to leave some things in the hands of almighty God. Even if we want to think in terms of productivity, if we burn ourselves out we become no good to the people we are trying to serve. More important than that, however, is that God loves you just as much as the people you are trying to serve. Your well-being is also important to the Lord.

Establishing appropriate boundaries in your work to help others is important. Once my wife and I were visiting some friends who lived amid these tensions. They worked hard to try to help others, but also had their own children and wanted to keep them safe. Their struggle started when an acquaintance asked to stay one night with them. Their friend was in dire straits, it was a cold winter night, and they knew this person and her story. She was sober and just needed a couch and a blanket. So they let her stay. A few weeks later she was back again, and they were happy to help once more. After some time, she came back with a few friends. They once again opened their home, but doing so became hard because they didn't know where to put this small group of people. The next time their friend showed up with an even larger group, and this time a bunch of them were intoxicated. My friends struggled with what to do. I don't remember what they did that particular night, but I remember that as they wrestled through their response, they came to the conclusion that they would offer their support only if they could do so out of love and not just guilt. They set their boundaries and stuck by them. This one woman would be allowed to sleep on their couch if needed, but her group of friends could find somewhere else to sleep, and nobody would be allowed in if they were drunk. The truth is, their relationship with this woman was becoming unhealthy. It was becoming less a friendship and more about enabling unhealthy behavior. Her relationship with them was becoming less and less about emergencies, and more about entitlement.

The reality is that there are times when people will try to take advantage of others. There are times when relationships become so unhealthy that their continued existence only further enables destructive behavior and burns people out. In such situations, it may be necessary to get some space from that relationship. In the next chapter we will talk about the powerful nature of healthy relationships, but that reality doesn't change the fact that we, at times, have unhealthy relationships that we must learn how to deal with wisely and carefully.

Everyone's situation is different, and we all must do the work of learning proper self-care. We also must learn to establish healthy boundaries in whatever context we find ourselves. Whether we live with a mental illness or are trying to help someone else suffering from one, we need to learn how to take care of ourselves. Whether we are experiencing addition or we care about someone struggling with it, if we want to maintain a healthy relationship, we also need to learn how to set healthy boundaries. It will be different for you than it might be for me, but it is important that we wrestle through these questions and come to some conclusions about what that will look like in our lives.

PART 3: **Fighting Poverty**

While we have touched on this subject already, this section of the book focuses on the question of "What now?"
How are we to live this out in our world? In the chapters
that follow, hopefully you will find some down-to-earth
advice about how to go about helping others, and some
stories that will warm your heart and challenge you
to put into practice some of the things we have been
talking about.

TEN

The Value of Relationships

IT WAS THAT TIME OF YEAR AGAIN. We all gathered around a table, and each person took a turn sharing with everyone who was gathered there. Most people had smiles on their faces as they talked and slight gleams in their eyes as they shared their thoughts with the rest of us. It was chilly outside and we were gathered around this table—nice, cozy, and warm. You might think I am talking about Thanksgiving or Christmas, but no: it was Roll Up the Rim season in Canada. This is the time of year when Tim Hortons gives out millions of prizes, from free coffee and donuts to large cash prizes and even free vehicles. It is almost a custom here to talk with those you are having coffee with about what you would do if you were to win the grand prize. Some wanted to pay off debt, some wanted to go on a vacation, others wanted a down payment for a house so they wouldn't have to continue renting. I sometimes joke that Roll Up the Rim is the only socially acceptable form of gambling for Christians.

As other people shared, my son, Marshall, was thinking about what he would do if he won the big cash prize. After giving it some thought, he said that he would want to "give the money to the poor people." I didn't correct him about using the term "poor people"—I don't much care for that term because of how it elevates poverty as a central piece of their identity. But Marshall was only six or seven years old and has always had a very compassionate heart, which was obvious to us since before he could talk. Once when he was only two, my wife was at a Mom's Morning Out program, and one of the childcare workers brought Marshall to her at the end of their time, explaining that if another child cried, Marshall would drop his toys, toddle across the room, and sit with them. It wasn't just that day, but every time he was there, and we were proud. So when he dreamed of giving his money to others, we smiled, loving that big heart of his. Giving away money, he thought, was the way to help people. They are poor, which in his mind means they don't have enough money. Therefore, the solution is simply a monetary one. He didn't just pull this idea out of a hat, either. He had witnessed us and people from our church giving away money, food, and gift cards many times. He had witnessed people on the streets asking for spare change. We don't often carry cash, so we would give some of our groceries if we had just come from a store, or offer to buy them a coffee, or get them a gift card from a local restaurant, or sometimes just sit and talk for a couple of minutes. Marshall always noticed people panhandling, even if we didn't.

It was striking that Marshall was the only one around the table who didn't talk about using the prize selfishly. The rest of us were absorbed in our own wants, desires, and even greed, but not him. The phrase from Isaiah comes to mind that says "And a little child will lead them" (Isaiah 11:6). I realize that this passage is not referring to my son, but he was leading us that day to remember those who are cold or hungry or need shelter. He didn't rebuke us for our selfishness, he simply thought in a different way, a better way, that gently reminded us of others and the importance of generosity. While this conversation revealed a blind spot within us about a lack of generosity, it also invites the question: Is giving money the only way to help? What if we didn't win the big cash prize and couldn't write a big check to charity? What about those of us who don't have a lot of spare income, and so are simply not able to help out financially? Does that mean that we are useless in helping reduce the poverty of those around us?

While I don't consider myself to be poor or to be someone truly living in poverty, I have usually lived below the poverty line set by Canada's government and community organizations. There were several times in my adult life when I thought I had finally made it above our poverty line, only to find out that the poverty line had moved because of inflation, and my family and I were still labeled "the working poor." Still, my children are growing up with far more creature comforts than I had as a kid, and even when I was young, we never had to sleep outside and we never missed a meal. I think it more realistic to use the global standards of poverty, which indicate that I am most definitely among the world's most wealthy. Even as a child we often had enough to share with others, and when we lost our home, we had a family member who took us in. The blessing of such relationships is huge, and I consider myself privileged in so many respects. While we have struggled to afford extras like music lessons without the help of government programs that provide them for free, our needs are met, and for that I am deeply thankful. So while we have and do give money to others, doing so often comes at a cost. It means we sacrifice something. Sometimes it means we sacrifice our trips to Tim Hortons for a while, other times it means we sacrifice money we were saving for a family trip. Because, in the words of my daughter Jasmine, "some things are just more important." Far too often, however, there are needs that are so much greater than the little bit of money that we can give.

Maybe you find yourself in a situation like me, where you can afford to give some money but wish you could do more. Or maybe you have greater monetary means and have given away lots of money but still feel that you aren't doing much. I have come to believe that time spent in relationship with others is just as important as giving money. Before discussing the value of such relationships, I should clarify something at the outset: Sometimes giving money is important, as that is what may be needed. I have been in need of such generosity and have received it. There is also the reality that while we in the Global North compare ourselves to one another and some of us feel poor by comparison, our spare change can feed a family in other parts of the world. So while we should not ignore the impact of a well-thought-out financial gift, for the average person, large contributions are simply out of the question. While we can and should give generously of whatever we are able to give, a huge part of what we can give is not only money, but friendship.

While money can and does make things happen, if we come back to the concept of poverty as a breakdown in various relationships, then having *healthy* relationships with others is both foundational and transformative in reducing poverty. This is not just a concept for a classroom—though I hope it is taught there too. It is an idea that has huge implications for everyday, grassroots kinds of work.

The YWCA in Kitchener, Ontario, created a program to help people experiencing homelessness transition into proper housing and self-sufficiency. These programs were quite successful at first glance, helping many people find both housing and employment. Over time, however, they found that some individuals whom the program had helped before would later come to be in need of the same help again. The program would provide housing and connect recipients with a suitable job, but after some time, many would return to the streets. While the more cynical people among us would shake our heads and dismiss the choices of these recipients as foolishness, their decisions were not without purpose. On the street these individuals had friends and a community. They would shiver in the cold together and sweat in the heat together. They would laugh together and cry together. After entering the program, however, they would go to work and come back to an empty home where they were lonely and isolated until they went to work again the next day; what was meant to be something good felt more like a prison. As their loneliness worsened, their longing for community grew, until they eventually left behind the comforts of their home and returned to the streets, where they at least had friends with whom to go through life. While the program was impressive on paper, it had a major blind spot in practice. What is truly impressive to me, however, was the program leaders' ability to honestly evaluate what was happening. They came to see that while their program was quite efficient and helpful, it was missing a key element that unraveled all their careful planning. Addressing poverty all came back to relationships. Messy, time-consuming relationships.

The program leaders asked Mennonite Central Committee to help, and they did. They developed a program called Circle of Friends, which connects people in this housing program with others who are committed to simply being friends.[1] These volunteers are not there to give money or to solve problems. They are there to be friends to these individuals who are lonely. The YWCA program became much more successful at transitioning people from homelessness to having a home and being self-sufficient, all because of the power of healthy, positive relationships. While money was needed for a while to help make this transition happen, it was the friendships that prevented it from unraveling and were central to the program's success.

Mother Teresa put it this way, "The greatest disease in the West today is not TB or leprosy; it is being unwanted, unloved and uncared for. We can cure physical disease with medicine, but the only cure for loneliness, despair, and hopelessness is love. There are many in the world who are dying for a piece of bread but there are many more dying for a little love. The poverty in the West is a different kind of poverty—it is a poverty not only of loneliness but also of spirituality. There's a hunger for love, as there is a hunger for God."[2] This is a profound observation that resonates deeply with Bryant Myers's view of poverty, and also with a trinitarian view of humanity as image bearers of the tri-une God; just as God exists in relationship between Father, Son and Holy Spirit, we also exist as relational beings, and so these relationships are an integral part of human flourishing.

Positive, healthy relationships are also key in breaking cycles of intergenerational violence. When a child is abused, there are a great many possible effects on the child's life. Some of the consequences include anxiety, depression, high levels of negative emotion, symptoms of post-traumatic stress, diminished ability to cope with new or stressful situations, aggression, and violent acting out in adulthood, among others.[3] Researchers have wondered why some abused children grow up to victimize others, while most in fact do not. While there are many factors involved in such a complex topic, one important factor was that those who didn't repeat the cycle had "a positive relationship with one of their parents while growing up."[4] While that single relationship didn't heal or eliminate all the negative consequences of abuse, it significantly mitigated them and was a huge factor in preventing the victimized child from becoming abusive to others as an adult. Across many studies they also consistently discovered the major positive impact of having just one posi-tive relationship with an adult, not necessarily a parent, "who will act as an advocate for him or her, who thinks he or she is wonderful and who accepts him or her unconditionally."[5] Even having just one healthy relationship with an adult friend made a significant difference in how resilient children became despite facing difficulties, and results became even more significant for children who had three or more positive adult relationships.[6] Once again, healthy relationships were credited with having a profound impact in the lives of many.

It will likely come as no surprise that positive relationships are also very important for mental and emotional health. As two social psychologists note, "Close and caring relationships are undeniably linked to health and well-being at all stages in the life span."[7] Their study talks about how relationships are important components to one's health, and vital for human thriving. They write, "Positive support not only helps buffer individuals from negative effects of stress, but also by enabling them to flourish either because of or in spite of their circumstances."[8]

From transitions from homelessness to self-sufficiency to dealing with addiction, from preventing abuse to improving mental and emotional health, healthy relationships can be trans-formative to the outcomes that people experience. The poverty of our world is not one of only money. To be clear, financial sup-port *is* important and often necessary, and I don't want to frame financial generosity as less important (more on that in the next chapter). Rather, I want to remind us here of the value and pow-er of healthy friendships. We should also remember that change doesn't happen overnight; it's not magic and it often feels messy. It can be painful and disorienting, discouraging, and upset-ting—yet it is this healthy connection with other human beings amid trials that makes a major difference in peoples' lives. As we talked about in chapter 9, there is a danger when relationships become unhealthy, where one person is only a "friend" if they can take advantage of the other person.

It is the powerful nature of relationships that gives them the potential to be dangerous or transformative. When they are unhealthy they can lead to all kinds of devastating outcomes. Think of the incredible damage that an abusive parent can do to their child that will last for a lifetime—or the power of a stable home and upbringing in helping children get a good start in life. When there are healthy relationships, people seem to flourish. The line between healthy and unhealthy can sometimes be hard to see, and when a relationship becomes unhealthy, people often wonder where the problems started or how it came to be that way. No relationship is perfect, after all. Yet the truth remains that in a healthy relationship, friendship can be a powerful force for good in the world, in a way that can be almost mysterious. It's like the value of a hug when you are feeling bad. What good does a hug do? Tangibly, not very much, yet sometimes that simple action from a friend can be powerful.

One Sunday morning I noticed out of the corner of my eye that someone from our congregation was crying. She quickly stepped into the coatroom. She had just arrived at church and hadn't yet spoken to anyone. Before I could do anything, one of our older women immediately went back there, simply to give our friend a hug. This older woman lived through dreadful poverty herself and is someone who deeply understands suffering. Her response to our friend was immediate and decisive, despite being self-conscious about her ability to speak English. I watched as the tears of the woman changed from tears of pain and loneliness to tears of thankfulness for the comfort. She hugged the older woman hard, as if in that moment this connection filled with compassion and love was all that was keeping her on her feet. While there was a bit of a language barrier between them, this action required no translation, and in that moment strength was given and received.

I am privileged and honored to say that I have watched countless moments like this in our church—real love given by real people that affects lives in powerful ways. Only God knows how our souls work, and while I don't know why they work the way they do, I know that following God's ways of love and compassion is powerful. I believe that there is a purpose and plan in God allowing us broken people to participate in the work of Christ, and that we are created for these kinds of powerful and transformative relationships. This kind of work is desperately needed in our world.

One Canadian reporter did a story about what Canada might be able to learn from the UK about loneliness. She reports, "Nearly half of Canadians say they are lonely, according to a new study from the Angus Reid Institute and Cardus. Britain considers loneliness an epidemic, and the government has even appointed a minister dedicated to the issue." There is increasing recognition that loneliness is a devastating problem in our world. Apparently, "loneliness is linked to a shorter life expectancy and in some cases is comparable to smoking fifteen cigarettes a day."[9]

Our world is in desperate need of people who are willing to simply be a friend to someone else. Not someone's savior, swooping in to save the day. Not a know-it-all who is condescending and judgmental. Not someone who thinks they are better than the other, and not an acquaintance who is little more than a walking ATM. Just a friend. What so many in our world need is simply another human being to see them as an equal and as someone with value, potential, and purpose. What is needed are more people who will be friends willing to know the other deeply and truly and to love them anyway.

As Christians this should be both a comfort and a call to action. It is a comfort because we don't have to have a lot of money to help others, which means we all can get involved. We don't have to have all the answers to other people's problems. After all, which of us has all the answers even to our own problems? What we can do is simply be a friend who listens, who values the other person, and who will be present. This should be a wake-up call to the church because a core piece of the gospel is that people can experience a healthy relationship with God, and also with one another. Jesus taught extensively about relationships, and this thread flows throughout the Scriptures from beginning to end. If the church believes the message that it proclaims, and if healthy relationships are so important to human flourishing, then it is, as they say, "a match made in heaven." This is truly good news!

Henri Nouwen writes, "As Jesus ministers, so he wants us to minister. He wants Peter to feed his sheep and care for them, not as 'professionals' who know their clients' problems and take care of them, but as vulnerable brothers and sisters who know and are known, who care and are cared for, who forgive and are being forgiven, who love and are being loved."[10] He continues, "We are not the healers, we are not the reconcilers, we are not the givers of life. We are sinful, broken, vulnerable people who need as much care as anyone we care for. The mystery of ministry is that we have been chosen to make our own limited and very conditional love the gateway for the unlimited and unconditional love of God. Therefore, true ministry must be mutual."[11] These are the kind of relationships that we ought to strive for, ones that become conduits for God's love and healing, and where none of us views ourselves as better than another.

We were sitting around the table, drinking coffee and listening to my son talk about how he would give away the prize money if he won the Tim Hortons Roll Up the Rim contest. While there are times when we need to give money, as Marshall wanted to do, there are other times when we should follow his example from his days at the Mom's Morning Out program: drop what we are doing and go and sit with those who are crying. In that moment in the restaurant, we were oblivious to the fact that what we already had, right then and there, was worth far more than the prize money and was making a far bigger difference than the cash we were all dreaming about. We had friends around the table, friends who have been there for one another through thick and thin. Friends who did in fact share money with one another, but more importantly friends who saw in the others not a project to be worked on and not a hero to be praised, but simply other human beings to be loved and cared for, regardless of how much or little money we had. As we continued our time at Tim Hortons, there was a sense of mutuality, even a sense of belonging, which really made us all the richest people in the room, even if our cups only said, "Please play again."

ELEVEN

Holistic and Sacrificial Giving

AS A CHILD I HEARD A STORY in a sermon about a small church that was collecting food items to give to a family in need. One of the congregants was a single mom with several children who was struggling to financially provide for her family all by herself. She contemplated whether she should bring anything; after all, she had her own children to provide for. She wanted to give generously, but knew it would mean her family would have to eat much more simply and forgo some other things in order to contribute. She began to "count her blessings," and knew that others in the world were in much more dire circumstances. So she gathered several bags of groceries together, giving all that she could, trusting that God would see them through. The prospect of not contributing left her feeling guilty, while the prospect of helping someone gave her a sense of joy and purpose. It wasn't a false guilt, but a deep sense of conviction as she tried to follow Jesus as best as she could. Well, she brought her several bags of groceries to church, and left it with the minister that

Sunday. Later that same day, she had a knock on her door, and she opened it up to see the minister and his wife standing there, groceries in hand for her and her children. After all that deliberation, the family the church wanted to bless was hers! And much to her surprise, half of the groceries given had originally come from her cupboards. In a stroke of great irony, she had donated more generously than anyone else in the church, while being the one the church wanted to help.

This story stuck with me all these years because of the many different lessons it teaches. It reminds us about the importance and virtue of giving sacrificially, even and especially when it costs us something. It reminds us that God provides for us even as we seek to help others. It also reminds us about how stingy many of us can be—how is it possible that the poorest member of that congregation contributed the most to this cause? This story includes a sharp rebuke about the lack of generosity that can sometimes be prevalent in our churches. What would happen if we all had the same attitude toward generosity as this single mother did?

In North America, the middle class is shrinking and many of us find it hard to pay our bills or continue the lifestyle to which our parents' generation was accustomed. Yet on a financial level, many in the Global North who live below the poverty line are still among the world's most wealthy people. In his book *Rich Christians in an Age of Hunger*, Ron Sider says, "One of the most astounding things about the affluent minority is that we honestly think we barely have enough to survive in modest comfort."[1] If we examine our lives, there are many things we could in fact do without in order to live more generous lives. Sider invites readers "to compare yourself with the poorest one-half of the world's people."[2] This can be a hard thing to do when we don't know people different from us. This surely is a stark reality to consider: even the amount of food we throw out each day in

North America could feed untold millions in other parts of the world. The bottom line is, I want to encourage you to consider giving generously and sacrificially to help others—but I also want to offer some important qualifications.

Global economies, inflation, and varying costs of living make this a rather big and complicated subject. The truth is, in places like the United States and Canada, the price of a cup of coffee can feed an entire family in other parts of the world. With our inflated cost of living compared to other places, we also have to make much more money to be able to buy even the basic necessities. Over the years I have personally not appreciated the guilt that is peddled to raise funds by some organizations, often in manipulative ways that are not always ethical. Yet there remains the simple fact that the scraps of the Global North would do a great deal to help the rest of the world precisely *because* of the varying costs of living. Child sponsorship programs have tapped into this, asking donors to give a modest amount of money to pay for schooling and food for a child in need in another part of the world. So on the one hand, when having these conversations we are sometimes made to feel unnecessary guilt over the amount of money we are required to earn in order to provide for our families.[3] On the other hand, because of the high cost of living, many of us have some measure of margin in our budgets and spending, so that even if we give a small amount, that small amount can go a lot further in other places around the world. We must also remember that many of us also live with far more luxuries than we need, and what we consider "needs" are often just frivolous extras. As you can see, these conversations are complex and multifaceted, leaving us with much to consider.

When it comes to financial giving, we all have many questions that we need to answer about where to donate money, how much to give, and our own attitudes when giving. While it is impossible for me to know where you are at personally, I want to encourage you to take a long, sober look at your own lifestyle, and to consider whether you ought to be more generous. For some of you, the answer will be an unequivocal and resounding yes. If that is the case for you, then the next step is to spend time considering the best place to donate your money. For others, however, the answer may not be as simple.

I have known people who feel such obligation and guilt around this issue that they give recklessly to others while neglecting the needs of their families and children. When contemplating this, some people can forget that God is also concerned for the well-being of them and their families, and they ought to stop giving so much away to others and take better care of their spouses, children, and parents. I have known people who give away thousands to charities and individuals on a whim but leave their own families penniless and in need. I have been surprised at how many people I've known who have lived this way. First Timothy 5:8 reminds us that "anyone who does not provide for their relatives, and especially for their own household, has denied the faith and is worse than an unbeliever." There are children who wished they were strangers to their parent, because then they might have received the care and compassion they needed. Ditto for some spouses and aging parents. Because they were family, their needs were therefore viewed as less important than the needs of strangers. Please don't get me wrong—your child or your spouse or your parents are not more valuable in the sight of God than an orphan overseas, but neither are they less valuable, and if they are under your care then you will be held to account someday for how you treat them, just as we will be asked about what we did for "the least of these" (see Matthew 25:31-46).

If you are someone who isn't taking proper care of those in your charge while being generous to others, then I beg you to stop giving so much to those causes until you learn to provide for those in your immediate care. If you are so busy caring for others that you don't properly care for your own family, then you have priorities that are not properly aligned with the Bible. In Mark 7:9-13, Jesus rebukes the religious leaders because they would encourage people to give even while neglecting family members for whom God desired them to care. Yet the leaders would accept the money and even encourage that kind of giving, knowing it would mean others would not be cared for. Jesus says that in doing this they nullified the word of God for the sake of their own tradition. In such cases, God has placed you in a position to help someone: your family. It is wrong to neglect that duty in order to help someone else or to further some other good cause. Caring for your aging parents, children, or spouse may not feel as glamorous as being involved in international work, but that doesn't mean it isn't important and holy work. Some folks who do fundraising might not appreciate me saying this, because it may mean that some people give less money to their cause. But don't feel guilty about being faithful in caring for the people God calls you to care for—and once you are doing that, then ask yourself what else you could do to help others.

I became friends with Calvin when he and I were both young men in our early years of vocational ministry, and we would get together often for long talks about theology, life, and ministry. He inspired me and challenged me. He's someone I greatly respected and looked up to—and I still do. One day we met at a local diner for lunch. This place didn't look like much, but their food was excellent. That day I noticed a bumper sticker slapped onto the back of his old station wagon, which said "Junky Car Club." It turned out that he had been inspired by the principles of simple living and generosity, so he joined this club, whose members were committed to driving modest vehicles instead of status symbols as a way to lower their cost of living to enable greater generosity. The bumper sticker also served as an amusing conversation piece—the club's motto was "Live with less so you can give more." While this club no longer exists, the concept of simplicity is a well-known historical distinctive of Anabaptist churches, where people are encouraged to live simpler lives that abandon materialism and consumerism. Unfortunately, sometimes I have watched as people embrace simple living but forget about the purpose behind it; they are not generous and instead focus on simply putting more money away for themselves. In our world, growing numbers of people are enthralled with the concept of minimalism, and their own lives improve as a result. While it can be healthy, in general, to "live with less," Christians are called to a greater purpose than only our own well-being. We are asked to also give to others. Simplicity for the sake of simplicity isn't necessarily any more virtuous than a life of excess. Simplicity for the sake of greater generosity, however, brings purpose and meaning that can be transformative not only for ourselves but for others as well.

When God spoke to Abraham, he said, "I will make you into a great nation, and I will bless you; I will make your name great, and you will be a blessing. . . . All peoples on earth will be blessed through you" (Genesis 12:2-3). We as the people of God are blessed, and are asked to bless others as well, just as God planned for Abraham. This is an ongoing trend throughout the pages of Scripture. God stated that Abraham was blessed in order to be a blessing to others, and this was meant to be a theme and principle in the life of an entire nation with regard to their relationship to the world. God sent Jesus to make a way for the salvation of all humanity, and God also has a plan for each and every person who becomes a child of the King. I love the passage that summarizes this by saying, "For it is by grace you have been saved, through faith—and this is not from yourselves, it is the gift of God—not by works, so that no one can boast. For we are God's handiwork, created in Christ Jesus to do good works, which God prepared in advance for us to do" (Ephesians 2:8-10). On the one hand, we are saved not by our works but by the simple yet profound grace of God. On the other hand, there is a plan and purpose for our lives, and there are good deeds we are invited to do as the children of God. Think of the language we so often use of the "body of Christ," where we all have different talents and play different roles in the work of Jesus in the world. In this biblical imagery, we are deeply connected to Jesus in all our diversity, and each part exists to serve a purpose. It doesn't have to earn its place in the body, but it is asked to perform its God-given function within that body.

When we talk about giving sacrificially, we often focus on the realm of finances; however I believe we do a tremendous disservice to this conversation when we keep our focus there. Yes, of course money is an important aspect of our lives that can be an effective tool to help others, and it is also true that Jesus taught about it a great deal. Yet when we talk about giving, we have so much more to offer than only our cash. We as people are much more than money-making machines—we have much more to offer, even while it is harder to quantify. Things like love, respect, friendship, and faith may be hard to fit onto a spreadsheet, but they are incredibly valuable for the healing of broken relationships that are at the root of poverty. In fact, I don't believe relationships can truly be healed without these elements.

I once attended a meeting where a community was wanting to create a multisector strategy to reduce or even eliminate poverty in their region. People were seated around tables, and periodically each table would have a small-group discussion where their thoughts would be recorded for future reference. As discussion progressed, I was surprised at how often people would start to dream about solutions that could actually transform the culture of neighborhoods and communities, where people would bring each other meals, check in on each other, share tools and services with each other, and simply be friends to one another to combat loneliness. They rightly observed the barriers people had because they didn't have access to goods or services that others might be able to share. As they dreamed, someone would eventually bring the group back to reality and say something like "That would be wonderful but that's more than what we can possibly accomplish. Let's focus on more practical ideas."

We had been strictly told that while pastors were invited to participate in this endeavor, any solutions were not to involve faith or religion. As an Anabaptist, I can appreciate the separation of church and state, yet I was dumbfounded by the irony, because the "pipe dream" that kept coming up about communities caring for each other as friends is the reality that I live out and witness every day in our church community. People who can't afford to buy their own tools borrow from others. Church members help each other in times of need, with everything from home renovations to car repairs to babysitting and home-cooked meals. We drive one another to doctor's appointments and cancer treatments and visit those who are lonely. We care for widows and single-parent families and help one another with paperwork related to immigration or health insurance. We sit with one another in courtrooms, in medical offices, and in funeral homes. Most of this care is organic and isn't part of any program, beyond our shared commitment to following Jesus. In our community, our faith is inseparable from these acts of love and care for each other.

I was left unsure of how to engage those community-level conversations, because the dreams that people had and dismissed as impossible are the everyday reality of our congregation. Yet the only reason this is our reality is because we are following Jesus, who invites us to love one another in such a holistic and practical way. The people in these meetings described their desires to experience these social benefits, but weren't interested in the

Jesus part. Yet Jesus is the reason why we give so sacrificially and holistically. While many outside our congregation experience some of these benefits because of the generosity of our congregation as they reach out and serve others, it is impossible for one small congregation to take care of an entire community alone. Interestingly, the roundtable gathering that day also included people who were receiving social assistance and who lived in poverty themselves. At the tables I was part of, these were also the people who vocally told everyone that we need Jesus in order to properly do what we were talking about. While I was initially thrilled that the meeting organizers brought these people in so they could "listen to the poor," I was saddened by how quickly the leaders dismissed and silenced them once they began to talk about faith, the very thing that is responsible for their "pipe dream" becoming a reality in my church community.

Regardless of your financial status, what do you have to give that could be a blessing to others? In a discipleship curriculum called *Holy Wanderings*, I wrote a chapter on simplicity and stewardship, in which I suggested that we have many assets at our disposal, such as power, time, skills, relationships, experiences, and yes, even money.[4] What would it mean for you to sacrificially give of your time, or what would it mean to offer your power? What would it mean to share your friendship or experiences? I would also like to suggest that you even have something a bit more unconventional to offer: your pain. There is something healing and restorative about vulnerability. Research professor Brené Brown has done a lot of groundbreaking work demonstrating that sharing our vulnerabilities and being open with our pain and insecurities can be transformative not only for our own lives but also for those around us—and even for organizational culture. Her work is inspiring, in part because it is contrary to the way we often think. Something about this concept seems to resonate deeply with the ways of Jesus. Henri

Nouwen writes, "The leaders of the future will be those who dare to claim their irrelevance in the contemporary world as a divine vocation that allows them to enter into a deep solidarity with the anguish underlying all the glitter of success, and to bring the light of Jesus there."[5] Nouwen suggests that it isn't in our successes that we affect the world but rather in walking with the broken and living in solidarity with those in pain. To do this requires us to be willing to enter the painful parts of our own being and to suffer alongside others while allowing Jesus to bring light into the darkness not just in ourselves but also in others.

So what do you have to offer others? Can you offer time by volunteering with a charity? Then serve joyfully. Are you good at quilting and want to use that as a way to bless others with quilts, or to raise money for an organization? Then sew cheerfully and put love into every stitch. Are you gifted with organization and helping with leadership? Consider serving on the board of directors for an NGO and helping with all the behind-the-scenes work that is needed to make things happen. Do you enjoy making friends and spending time with people over coffee or tea? Then consider getting involved with a program that visits those who are housebound or lonely, or simply take the time to chat with people you meet on the street. Maybe you're not good with people but you still want to help: well, organizations ranging from homeless shelters to food banks need janitors just like any facility, and you could volunteer to simply mop some floors and empty some garbage cans. Whatever you have to offer, offer it generously, and with joy in your heart. This isn't a new concept at all; it is what the apostle Paul instructs when he says, "We have different gifts, according to the grace given to each of us. If your gift is prophesying, then prophesy in accordance with your faith; if it is serving, then serve; if it is teaching, then teach; if it is to encourage, then give encouragement; if it is giving, then give generously; if it is to lead, do it diligently; if it is to show mercy, do it cheerfully" (Romans 12:6-8). Don't feel guilty for all the things that you can't do. Don't harangue yourself about all the talents that you don't have. Simply take a serious look at yourself with "sober judgment" (v. 3) and then be faithful to the Lord with what you have been given, and give to others sacrificially and generously.

TWELVE

Turn Off the Tap

MY WIFE'S SISTER ERIN attended Canadian Mennonite University in Winnipeg around the same time that I attended Providence University College, only a forty-five-minute drive away. My wife and I would often make the trip up to the city with our little ones to visit her, and as we sat and visited, the content of our studies would often come up. Erin was in the International Development program, so we often talked about issues surrounding poverty and development. She has always been a brilliant thinker with an excellent memory and has the incredible ability to share her thoughts in ways that are both engaging and memorable. On one such visit we were again talking about poverty, and the sheer magnitude of needs in the world. Erin shared an analogy that had come up in one of her classes that has stuck with me ever since. It is a somewhat disturbing mental picture, but it was apt in making its point.

Imagine, if you will, that you are standing at the base of a large skyscraper. As you look up, you realize that you can't even see the top of this building, but suddenly you see something falling. At first you want to duck for cover, until you realize that it's a baby. You rush to catch this poor little babe, and do so, dramatically saving its life. Then you see another, and then another, and you and the rest of the crowd at the base of this building get to work catching these little ones lest any one should perish. This continues for a time, but nobody goes to the top of the building to see why and how so many babies are falling off, and why it won't stop. Such, Erin explained, is the nature of development work. There are dire needs that are immediate, and the consequences of not helping may result in someone's demise—there are literally countless scenarios where the stakes are life-and-death. Yet there are problems and issues that go beyond what we can immediately see, and if we could address those systemic causes, we might be able to stem the tide of such peril. Typically, that means using resources to figure out what's going on instead of addressing the needs right in front of us that are incredibly urgent.

Ron Sider has shared a similar analogy. As the story goes, in India there once was a mental health facility for people who had lost their sanity, and the facility had a method for determining whether someone's sanity had returned to them. They set the patient in front of a tub of water, which also had a tap that was turned on, putting ever more water into the tub. They gave the individual a spoon and then asked them to empty the tub. Some would simply begin emptying the tub one spoonful at a time, without first turning off the tap. This was an indication that the patient was not ready to go home. Those who first turned off the tap before beginning the task of scooping water had a sufficient grasp of reality, and therefore they were allowed to leave.[1]

What both of these stories illustrate is the importance of getting to the root of the problem, instead of simply treating the symptoms. The first analogy illustrates how difficult it can be to get to the root cause of the problems when the symptoms are disastrous and the stakes are high.

Thankfully, poverty doesn't always pose either/or scenarios. We don't always have to choose *either* to treat the symptoms *or* to address the root cause. While there are, of course, exceptions, for many the symptoms can be addressed while also addressing the root of the problem. This, however, can be incredibly challenging, especially when the root causes of poverty are often relational. As I described in chapter 1, Bryant Myers lists the types of relationships in four categories: between people and God, others, themselves, and their environment.[2] Wayne Gordon and John Perkins, in *Making Neighborhoods Whole*, make another helpful distinction. When talking about reconciliation between people, they distinguish between reconciling "people with other people, and people groups with other people groups."[3] This distinction adds an important layer of nuance, because the way one approaches the restoration of relationships between two individuals is different from the way one approaches restoring relationships between groups—for instance, between ethnic groups, religious groups, or even between certain groups and the government.

So how do we get to the root of the problem in order to help people? Well, the first step is to establish a relationship with someone with enough mutual trust so that we can listen and find out what's going on. This alone is a huge commitment, as it often takes time to build trust in order to know who a person is, where that person has come from, and the various culminating factors that resulted in their poverty. Furthermore, if an individual does not want to have a friendship or relationship of that nature, then that lack of interest really curtails such efforts—and respecting the person's wishes in this regard is also an important piece of recognizing basic human dignity. If someone doesn't want to be friends, you cannot force a friendship. And if someone wants only an *unhealthy* relationship, then that, too, is detrimental. The reality is, there are some instances when people would rather have only their symptoms addressed instead of addressing the root causes of their poverty. At other times people will gladly do whatever it takes as long as they know that the people who are trying to help them care, and that they will stick around through the process. These two positions, of course, represent only two ends of a spectrum, and they are also not mutually exclusive. There are people who will ask only for their symptoms to be addressed, but who would also be willing to do what it takes to address the cause if only someone would be there with them through it. Sometimes, however, these individuals have been hurt by others who abandoned them in the past, and they remain deeply skeptical of such efforts because of how people seeking to help sometimes give up when things get tough.

Assuming you have a healthy relationship with the person you are trying to help, and assuming you know a sufficient amount about the person and the situation, then the key to "turning off the tap" is to find out what breakdown in relationships resulted in such poverty. Consider the situation of someone whom I will call Susannah. When I first met her she was a teenager who had run away from home and was couch surfing with friends. In time, she had to deal with homelessness, addiction, and more. Susannah had run away from home because of a breakdown in the relationship with her parents. The pain of this and the difficulty of homelessness led to substance abuse and other dangerous activities as a way of numbing the pain. One day she asked to talk to my wife and me. We did very little but listen to her and her story. The reason she wanted to talk was because she had spiritual questions. So we shared with her the good news of Jesus, and that day she accepted the salvation offered through Christ, giving her heart to the Lord. I would like to tell you that this solved all her problems, but it didn't, and because of a variety of circumstances, it would be a long time until we saw her again. While there most definitely was a spiritual poverty that needed healing, the root cause of her physical poverty was the broken relationship between her and her parents. While my wife and I had a relatively new friendship with her, we had no relationship with her family, and there seemed to be very little we could do.

Susannah had an adult friend who was also friends with Susannah's parents, and who in the end did a lot to help mediate their conflict and facilitate healing for that relational brokenness as well—to the point that Susannah was eventually able to return home. So while I am glad that she became a Christian, it did not immediately solve her problems, though it did help give her strength to go through a program at an addiction recovery center, and also helped her do her part in healing the relationship between her and her parents. In Susannah's case, the problem wasn't only addictions or dangerous activities. It wasn't only the hunger in her belly or the lack of shelter. While many of these symptoms did in fact need treatment, a broken relationship was at the center of this, fueling the poverty that had overtaken her life. This story illustrates the difficulty of finding the root cause of poverty, but even more than that, the difficulty of helping people find healing for these broken relationships.

There is one beloved older woman in our congregation whom many of us affectionately refer to as "Grandma." She speaks very little English, though she does okay with understanding the basics. Thankfully, her relatives in our congregation are able to translate when necessary. This lovely woman had some health problems and was in need of minor surgery to help. The problem, however, was that she didn't have any health insurance, so she had to pay out of pocket for the procedure, which was several thousand dollars. In Canada, we have a form of socialized healthcare for anyone who is a citizen or permanent resident. Yet there are cases where someone may be in the country legally, but not have medical coverage. This was the case for Grandma. As

I spoke to her family in our congregation, I found out that this had been normal for her since immigrating, which was troubling because she was in fact legally entitled to Canadian citizenship—though she didn't have it.

The first thing we did was plan a fundraiser to raise money for her to have the procedure done. While we weren't able to raise quite enough to cover it all, it was enough to allow her to go forward with the procedure. Grandma had lived most of her life in Mexico, but when most of her family moved to Canada, she decided to move to Canada as well to be with them. While she was legally entitled to Canadian citizenship, a mistake made in her paperwork in Mexico years ago meant that her information didn't align with the information held by the Canadian government. So while she was entitled to citizenship, and therefore healthcare, the governmental red tape around the paperwork prevented that from happening. The more I got involved, the more hopeless it seemed, as it seemed every avenue for pursuing her citizenship was exhausted. We tried to help and failed, and so we fervently prayed to God, not knowing what else to do.

My theological beliefs really rail against my statement, by the way—praying fervently only after failing in my own efforts. I wish my practice lined up more with my beliefs in this instance, because fervent prayer should have been the first thing I did. In any case, we prayed and prayed for several months. It felt hopeless. While we believed that God would take care of her, it seemed that there was nothing we could do, because the law prevented from happening what should have happened. Then we got the news. A minor law had been changed at the federal level that now enabled the immigration office to cut through the bureaucracy and allow Grandma to finally become a Canadian citizen. Furthermore, a bunch of her medical debt was forgiven retroactively because she had been entitled to citizenship all along. In situations like this, I find Shane Claiborne's words so profound:

"We believe despite the evidence, and then we watch the evidence change."[4] We believed that God would care for Grandma despite all the evidence that seemed to squash all hopes of ongoing medical care, yet in the end the evidence changed and we saw her needs met, and we continue to praise the Lord for this because she has had other medical needs since then.

In this instance, the broken relationship was between Grandma and the government, where there was a systemic problem that created inequality for her. It wasn't that the government was trying to swindle her out of what she was entitled to; it was that this problem in paperwork made it impossible to follow policies and laws while also granting her citizenship. I am thankful that the law was changed to enable officials to address her circumstances with justice and equity.

There are many times when systems and structures are at the root of problems. Shane Claiborne shared a story with me about Miss Betty, a woman he knew whose kitchen was destroyed by a small fire, although the rest of the home survived.[5] The government had grants to help with the restoration of her kitchen, so she applied for one. Meanwhile, child welfare officers found out she didn't have a kitchen, so they took away her grandchildren who lived with her. To add insult to injury, her grant application was denied because they gave priority to families with children in the home—and since her grandchildren were taken away she was now considered only a single person. Such situations demonstrate that the brokenness of our systems can cause, or at least exacerbate, poverty in people's lives. To quote Martin Luther King Jr., "One day we must come to see that the whole Jericho Road must be transformed so that men and women will not be constantly beaten and robbed as they make their journey on life's highway. True compassion is more than flinging a coin to a beggar. It comes to see that an edifice which produces beggars needs restructuring."[6]

In cases of systemic causes of poverty, where governments and officials have something to do with the cause, the solution may in fact be to simply alert the authorities to the problem, and if that doesn't work, to challenge them to make it better. Sometimes even knowing and being able to contact the correct authority who has the power to help—and having the courage to get in touch—is an immense privilege and a source of power in our world. There are times when sharing our privilege and power may involve respectfully advocating for our friends who are in need or, even better, helping them advocate for themselves.

Also consider the many, many stories globally of the poverty within entire nations, as a direct result of broken relationships between leaders and people that resulted in years of war and bloodshed. For a great many of these countries, the brokenness can be traced back further to colonial domination that destroyed their cultures and systems of government and enslaved people for generations, causing undue suffering for centuries because of unjust laws and discriminatory policies. Such historical damage is of course among the most difficult to bring healing to, and any naive or trite response can end up doing far greater damage than good.

There are also times when poverty is the direct result of a person's own bad decisions or self-destructive practices. There is such a thing as laziness, and the Bible does also warn against it: "Lazy hands make for poverty, but diligent hands bring wealth" (Proverbs 10:4). This is a real problem for some people, and when this is the case, the solution is to learn how to work. Yet I want to warn you: while this may be true for some, it is rare in my experience for this cause to exist in complete isolation; it usually exists in tandem with other broken relationships. I have known people who failed to pass their courses in high school or in university who were obsessed with video games. They loved the fantastical realities in their games more than they enjoyed the real world, so whenever they got the chance they would escape from the pressures of reality into a world of fantasy where they could delve into exciting stories and captivating adventures and the worst thing that could happen was to have to start the level over again. Captivating indeed, because these games constantly held their minds hostage. This obsession led some to live in poverty because they would stay up late into the night playing these games, making them unable to get up in the morning and function in the real world. Eventually the real world became more and more difficult for them, and the escapist mindset became their norm, which led to financial ruin. In such cases, something in their life left them dissatisfied with the world they were in and their role in it. Perhaps they felt powerless over something and these games allowed them to feel powerful. They had a broken relationship with themselves and how they viewed themselves as unable to embark on real adventures, and even a broken relationship with their environment—perhaps not the environment in a physical sense, but in a way that failed to see the world and their existence in it as a good thing.

Far too often, people assume that most poverty is because of laziness. They read passages like the one quoted above about laziness resulting in poverty and come to believe that the reverse is true: poverty is therefore the result of laziness. Making such assumptions is destructive, and can damage relationships before they even begin. For most people in poverty, their poverty is the result not of laziness but of other complicated factors. Conversely, some people have immense financial wealth while having very little work ethic. One summer between my years of university, I spent some time working in the oil fields in Alberta, helping with some environmental services. During this time, I heard a work philosophy that some of the other workers embraced: "Hide-and-seek for three grand a week." Many of the workers made more in a month than I did that whole summer, and they hated their jobs, so as soon as their immediate supervisor turned his back, they would hide behind a large holding tank somewhere and smoke and visit or take naps until their supervisors found them. Workers were in short supply in those days so such behavior was tolerated, but this proved to me that the most lazy people in our society are not necessarily those who have nothing; the sin of laziness also lurks in the hearts of many people who have lots of money. While I certainly believe in the power of hard work, I also believe that this should not generally be a concern we have for people in poverty; in my experience this is rarely the root issue, and as such it would be foolish to assume when trying to help reduce poverty. Even the folks I've known over the years who "play the system" to try to get as many free resources as they can typically do far more work to obtain their "free" resources than they would if they worked for them, even at minimum wage.

While we may need to address the symptoms of poverty, we must also peel back its layers in order to uncover the root causes, and to discover which relationships are in need of healing. This requires time, honest and open relationships, trust, love, and much more. The root cause or causes are usually as unique as the person who is in poverty, which is why "one size fits all" solutions are often not as helpful as we would like. So the bad news is that this is complicated and sometimes confusing, but the good news is that authentic and healthy relationships go a long way toward helping untangle the web of circumstances to figure out the true causes of the poverty and the symptoms of that problem. Often there are no quick-and-easy solutions, but in cases where there is a course of action to address the root cause of a person's poverty, you may be able to help that person walk the road to healing and out of poverty.

I want to recognize that some of the examples in this chapter may leave you with a sense of hopelessness. First, it is important to recognize that we may not actually be able to solve all the world's problems, and there may be times when our only possible response is to lament the pains in our world like the psalmists in the Bible. Second, and more importantly, while we may not always be able to see a way through a particular circumstance, there is always reason to have hope. We may not be the saviors of the world or know how to fix a particular problem, but God sees the difficulties around us and truly cares. We serve a God who has the ability to make "a way in the wilderness and streams in the wasteland" (Isaiah 43:19). It is vitally important that we recover a sense of hope for the future if we are to have success with making that future a reality in our world. God made us with free will and with the ability to have agency in our own lives, and this truth can help us rediscover a true sense of hope for tomorrow, even if our yesterdays look pretty bleak. My friend Mark Dalley from the Salvation Army says that building hope back into people's lives is crucial before anything else can happen. The story of Jesus and the salvation we read about in the Bible offers us a hope that extends into eternity, and it also gives us a vision for what is possible here on earth when we choose to live out God's will "on earth as it is in heaven" (Matthew 6:10).

THIRTEEN

Choice and Consequence

THEY WERE TOO STUNNED TO CRY. Both the father and the mother sat in silence for a while, and the father's face started turning red. I knew him well enough to know that he was getting angry, which was only a cover for his extreme grief. Their teenage child had made some very self-destructive decisions that had some significant ramifications. Again.

While my children are still quite young, I have had to watch friends, family, congregants, colleagues, coworkers, and mentors go through such situations. As parents, they feel it is their job to guide, lead, and teach their children—which of course it is. Yet as their children become adults, they must make their own decisions and live with the consequences of their choices, even when those choices hurt their loved ones. The parents usually say something like "But we taught them better than this . . ." as their voices trail off and they sit in anguish. And they did teach them better. Watching children walk away from the values, faith, or virtues you sought to instill in their hearts is excruciating and heart-wrenching.

The reality is, however, that while people can exert some measure of influence on others, at some point every person has to make their own choices by which they will flourish or flounder. I have known many people who have found some measure of comfort in remembering that Jesus, who was God incarnate, even had a disciple, Judas, who made a choice that resulted in Jesus' unjust and murderous crucifixion. Then there is the story of Adam and Eve, two people who saw God face-to-face and who walked with God in paradise, yet who chose to do something that resulted in their exile from the garden of Eden. The free will that each person possesses is a powerful force. While we may not all have the same power or influence in our world, the same amount of wealth or the same opportunities, we all have the same capacity for exercising free will. The consequences may not always be the same, thanks to things such as varying amounts of privilege or power—sometimes even because of corruption—but the power to take control of our own choices and actions is a universal human ability, regardless of status, wealth, or privilege.

I have known people who have gone through terrible trauma and lived most of their lives in underprivileged and oppressive circumstances, yet rose above things like abuse, mental illness, racism, lack of education, poverty, and so much more to become healthy and generally happy individuals. I have also watched as people are given everything they could ask for on a silver platter, yet throw their lives away and make choices that inevitably result in poverty and all kinds of suffering. Other times people who grew up with wealth and privilege take full advantage of the opportunities given them and become understandably successful. Still other times, individuals may feel so powerless because of how they have been brutally oppressed or victimized that they forfeit their free will—consciously or subconsciously—to their trauma and continue in cycles of abuse and poverty.

Something that truly bothers me is that many people who come from places of power and privilege speak in condescending ways about free will. Those of us who have experienced poverty or abuse or oppression or injustice do, in fact, have the power to make good and bad choices; however, this truth is sometimes touted in a way that is devoid of compassion, understanding, and love. This topic, more than many, is one that must be handled with care. The truth about the power of our choices can, in fact, be life-changing for those who embrace it. Yet the way in which this truth is often delivered can be without respect or love. It is sometimes even used as a means of dismissing one's duty toward others. So while I theologically and philosophically embrace the idea that we all have inherent power over our own choices and actions, I have often been appalled by how some use this truth as a way to avoid helping others or to arrogantly build themselves up and cast judgment on those who have less.

Some of the perversions of this truth may sound like this: "Look at how successful I am; it is the result of my own hard work. If other people only worked as hard as I did, then they too would be successful." Or like this: "It's their choice to be poor because of their poor decisions." Or even like this: "Why should I give my own hard-earned money to fix their mistakes? If they made those choices before they will make them again, so it's no use to try to help." Notice how each statement carries with it a grain of truth, but also carries stigma, arrogance, and ignorance? Like many things, complete lies are not always as destructive, because they are easier to recognize as untrue. Half-truths are usually far more destructive than outright lies because they are poison pills with only a veneer of truth to make them palatable. The words of Jesus here are as insightful as they are practical as we try to sort this out: "Watch out for false prophets. They come to you in sheep's clothing, but inwardly they are ferocious wolves. By their fruit you will recognize them" (Matthew 7:15-16).

Conversations about free will should not become conversations that are used to be condescending toward others or as a way of dismissing others. Nor should free will be denied because of some misguided sense of "knowing better" than the people you supposedly want to help. Properly talking about the power of one's own choices is something that can and should bring dignity back to the conversation. It should be something that empowers others instead of further stripping them of power.

To speak in a modern parable, imagine with me, if you will, that there were three brothers who were raised in poverty and were severely abused from the time they were children—and all of whom found an escape through substance abuse. They felt powerless their whole lives because they had largely been powerless. For years they lived a life of poverty and felt incredibly hopeless. After years of addiction, the first brother decided to make a change, and went to an addiction recovery program. It was the hardest time of his entire life, living without the substances that numbed him to his pain and, furthermore, having to confront the many painful memories of his past. He was also confronted with his own mistakes and sought to make restitution for the ways he had also hurt others. After he graduated from the program, he got a job, continued to do his work to remain sober, and his life slowly began to improve.

The second brother saw this and became bitter. He assumed that the first brother felt superior because of his sobriety. He missed his brother, who used to come over and drink with them, and who now largely stayed away because of the constant presence of alcohol. He felt betrayed and added this to his long list of other betrayals in his life, and went further into his addictions.

The third brother, however, responded differently. He saw that the first brother was able to conquer his addiction, yet also went through just as much difficulty as they had. So the third brother thought, "Maybe I can do it too." He was happy for his brother to get out of the misery of addiction and to begin to live a life that wasn't so strongly marked by poverty and suffering. While he was jealous of him, which was difficult for their relationship, it planted the seed of possibility regarding the power of his own choices. He too made the choice to get sober, and with the help of the first brother eventually did so.

While this story is fictional, it is representative of what I have watched repeatedly play out in a variety of circumstances. From crippling addictions to hurting marriages to living with mental illness, individuals can make choices that can help them or harm them. The way one responds to challenges can make all the difference in the outcome. Even the most destitute of people has been given great power through the gift of free will.

Greg Pearson from The Bridge, an urban ministry in Saskatoon, Saskatchewan, says, "Most people that come to us because of their impoverishment have no sense of volitionality [free will]. There's no sense of choice in their life. Yes, they have been victims. But they have also chosen to *not* seek help. One of the things we really try to do is to help people reestablish that sense of choice, and out of that comes life skills and hope and all those other things."[1] When the people seeking their help rediscover that there are some things that they do in fact have control over, they realize that they are not just powerless and voiceless victims of the tragedies that befell them. They begin to realize that despite their victimhood, they still have some things left within their control. Regaining a sense of power over their own lives enables them to dream and hope for the future, and to learn to think about what they can do to improve their state instead of merely lamenting what others are not doing for them or the harm they were powerless to prevent in the past. This helps recapture that sense of hope for a better future that we so desperately need as we try to make our world a better place.

When working with people in poverty, one of the most powerful things one can do is to help reestablish, as Pearson suggests, their sense of free will in a way that is compassionate and loving, not using such ideas to dismiss them or control them, but rather to empower them and enable them to help solve their own problems. They will likely be unable to do everything themselves (who of us can?), but it will encourage folks to do their part.

This is part of the rationale for organizations who offer microloans to people in poverty. Instead of merely giving away money and supplies as handouts, they offer small loans to people seeking to start small businesses. In one possible scenario they might loan someone money to buy chickens so they can sell eggs, or to buy a cow so they can sell milk and cheese. The individuals receiving the support are then required to invest it wisely so they can pay it back. In the end, those who receive these loans end up paying them back, making their businesses something they truly did of their own free will. Rather than being a handout, the loan becomes a hand up. Imagine the sense of accomplishment and dignity after they make their last payment, knowing that their business is now theirs and theirs alone and that they deserve the credit for the hard work of making this success possible. Without a sense of free will and a hope for a better tomorrow, these organizations would not be able to function and their model would flop. In general, however, this approach has seen a lot of success because valuing the power of an individual's choices can be tremendously uplifting and dignifying for people. In the words of urban ministry founder Robert Lupton, "The poor, no matter how destitute, have enormous untapped capacity; find it, be inspired by it, and build upon it."[2]

Moses Maimonides was a twelfth-century Jewish philosopher and Torah scholar who created a framework now referred to as "Maimonides's ladder of tzedakah," which talks about differing forms of charity. The lower rungs of this proverbial ladder are inferior forms of charity in comparison to the higher rungs of the ladder. Near the bottom of this ladder are forms of charity where people give begrudgingly. Further up the ladder, people give joyfully, and even with varying levels of anonymity. He includes considerations about having to be asked to give or offering to give of one's own accord. At the top of the ladder, however, is where people have business partnerships with those in need, so that it empowers those in need to work to provide for themselves. This is seen as the most noble form of charity, because of how it respects the dignity of the person in need. Sadly, this ancient wisdom is all too often neglected.

One of the hard parts about free will is watching someone walk away or watching someone fail. Steve Corbett and Brian Fikkert, in *When Helping Hurts*, believe, "Do not do for people what they can do for themselves."[3] As Corbett and Fikkert write about development endeavors, they even recommend that if the people they are serving don't carry out their own responsibilities, development workers should "not step in and take up those responsibilities."[4] While stepping in and doing something for others that they can and should do for themselves might make the work appear more successful, the danger is that it fosters a sense of dependency and does not foster the sense of ownership that needs to be present in an individual's or community's life in order to cultivate long-term wellness.

A remarkable double standard persists: on the one hand we dismiss the needs of others because we think they should be able to "pull themselves up by their own bootstraps." On the other hand, when we engage in poverty reduction work where we foster unhealthy dependency, we undercut people's own free will for the sake of our efforts looking more successful, and we end up robbing people of the power of their own choices, which is one of their greatest resources in battling their own poverty.

A story in the Bible offers a lot of food for thought when it comes to the topic of free will and the power of our own choices. The gospel of Luke recounts the parable of the prodigal son (Luke 15:11-32). Jesus tells his followers about a man who had two sons, one of whom asked his father for his share of the inheritance. Strangely, the father grants this request—he doesn't refuse this foolish desire but gives the son an early inheritance. The son then moves far away and completely squanders his wealth on what Jesus calls wild living. Then famine strikes the land and this young man goes from a life of lavish excess to a life of destitute poverty, going so far as to envy herds of swine because they at least have food to eat. In the end, the son returns home to a father who graciously takes him back and showers him with love.

One of the things that I used to find troubling was the actions of the father. How could a father grant the request of his son and give him his inheritance? Didn't he know his son well enough to know it would be wasted? Shouldn't he have declined to do this? While I could easily understand how this parable points us to a loving God who takes us back after we have acted foolishly and sinfully, I had a harder time understanding how this father was acting in a way that was loving when he allowed his son to move away and throw away all his wealth so foolishly. You see, the father in this story, like God, allowed for free will. The father surely taught his son better, but still allowed his son to make his own life choices even if they resulted in poverty. This free will is part and parcel of healthy relationships. If there is no free will, then it is not true relationship but rather obligation or even slavery. Yet a loving and healthy relationship requires free will and allows people to walk away, even when it is detrimental to themselves. It is true that freedom of choice is responsible for the existence of evil perpetrated by people in the world; yet it is also what makes possible the existence of love.

The apostle Paul offers some powerful instructions when he says, "Do not repay anyone evil for evil. . . . but overcome evil with good" (Romans 12:17, 21). While we may not be able to control what others do to us, Paul in this passage assumes and outright commands that we take responsibility for how we respond to such evil. Jesus also instructs us to love our enemies, which points to our God-given ability to act in accordance with something other than instincts, and our innate ability to choose our responses despite what we may feel like doing. In properly embracing volition, we can begin to sow seeds of love where there had been seeds of scorn. We can begin to sow seeds of forgiveness and freedom where there had been roots of bitterness. We can allow God to turn the deserts of our hearts into gardens and the wastelands into life-giving soil, and we can invite others into this transformative way of being as well.

When we abandon our own freedom of choice, we abandon our greatest asset in the fight against our own poverty. When we serve others without respecting their choices and will, we do an inherent disservice because we are no longer treating them with dignity, and even more importantly, we are no longer treating them with the same respect that God gives us to make our own choices. Unfortunately, when we embrace the value of free will, our endeavors to help others may fail miserably, not through any fault of our own but because those we seek to help walk away or act in destructive ways. Yet only in the context of valuing the free will of others can our efforts succeed in the truest sense. Despite the risk of evil and hatred, God saw fit to endow us with our own agency, all for the sake of love. Likewise, despite the risks of having less measurable success, allowing people to make their own choices and showing dignity by valuing their free will is what opens the door to making a lasting and meaningful impact in people's lives. It is in this context that we can truly recover a hope for a better tomorrow and then begin taking steps to make that possibility a reality.

PART 4: **Risks and Possibilities**

So we have come to understand that we are supposed to be doing God's good work in this world, and we have been given some tools and encouragement and are excited to get to work. Before we jump in, we should ask what might happen as we get involved. What can we expect when we serve the Lord in this way? Well, for starters we might end up hurting people. We might fail. When that happens, we can choose to give up or to "fall forward" and learn from our mistakes. We might see small acts accomplish something amazing, and we might see a lot of big acts do only small things. We also might see big actions do big things and small actions do small things. It might even appear that many actions have seemingly no impact at all at first glance. In this section we consider what might happen once we get involved.

FOURTEEN

When We Harm

"A GREAT MARRIAGE IS the union of two forgivers." These words from the couple standing at the podium struck me as profound so I jotted them down as quickly as I could. My fiancé and I were attending a seminar for engaged couples and there was a lot of talk about conflict, forgiveness, and what to do when we hurt each other. I wasn't as naive as some people; I knew marriage had challenges. In fact, by the ripe old age of five I told my mother I wouldn't get married, because "it just doesn't work." I eventually grew out of such a skeptical approach, and would soon be married to Emily Weaver, a woman whose family hailed from Lancaster County, Pennsylvania. Because I come from a Russian/Mexican Mennonite background, and Emily from the Swiss Mennonites of Pennsylvania, we had many excellent conversations about our different cultures and faith convictions. We both knew that marriage could be difficult at times, but throughout our engagement we heard comments from other engaged couples wondering why these seminars focused so much on conflict and forgiveness. "But we're in love! It's not like we are enemies!" The friends who spoke such things usually were the ones with a particularly difficult first year of marriage. What we knew intellectually but would soon learn firsthand is that we often hurt most those whom we love the most. This was the reason for so much education and discussion about conflict as we prepared for marriage. It turns out, the closer a relationship one has with someone, the more we can demonstrate love in ways that they understand, but the greater capacity we have to cause them pain. In marriage we let someone into the depths of our heart, into the fragile and beautiful places of our very soul, to be a companion who will cry with us, and marvel at the beauty we had forgotten existed. And sometimes marriage is like tripping while in this place; falling over in a most undignified way, flailing and grabbing and clutching at whatever we can to break our fall, only to realize we are surrounded by crowded shelves of delicate glass ornaments—many of which come crashing down during this terrible spectacle. In marriage, they say it is not a matter of *if* you hurt each other, but *when*.

Since people enter into marriage without a clue about how they will hurt their spouse, it is no wonder that so many of us also seek to reduce poverty without giving a thought to the fact that our efforts might result in causing harm to the people we are trying to bless. This isn't a concept about which the Bible is ignorant, either. The writer of Proverbs says, "If anyone loudly blesses their neighbor early in the morning, it will be taken as a curse" (Proverbs 27:14). What this proverb gets at isn't some over-spiritualized teaching about curses, but rather something much simpler. Sometimes the things we do to try to do good can in fact be unappreciated when done in a certain way. Imagine it is Christmas morning, and your overly cheery neighbor comes by your house and rings your doorbell repeatedly, making you think something urgent and important is going on. You are startled awake, and in your bleary-eyed state try to find your bathrobe. The doorbell keeps ringing, and you stumble through your house, turning on lights as you go, reach the door, and open it to discover your neighbor standing there in his ugly Christmas sweater. You ask him what's wrong, and he says with a huge grin, "Nothing's wrong! I just wanted to say Merry Christmas!" You mumble a response, politely thank him, and then close the door, irritated at how your neighbor is so obnoxious, and in a way that makes him think that he's actually being a good neighbor. This is what this proverb is getting at, and this is unfortunately how so many of us can be when we blindly seek to make the world a better place. The motives are excellent, but the methods are sometimes less than stellar. Robert Lupton, author of *Toxic Charity*, observes, "We mean well, our motives are good, but we have neglected to conduct care-full due diligence to determine emotional, economic, and cultural outcomes on the receiving end of our charity."[1]

A few years ago, someone from our church heard of a family who recently immigrated to Canada from Mexico who was struggling financially to get back on their feet. This family didn't have much at all, and it was Christmastime. The mother of this family had lamented to her friend in our church that they didn't even have enough money to have a special Christmas dinner as a family. Moved by compassion, we organized a collection of gifts for their children, and many groceries—including all the fixings for a special Christmas dinner. As our church people went to deliver these gifts that were gathered with such love, the mother and the children were ecstatic, just as we had all hoped they would be. But the father of this house was not so appreciative. He wasn't rude, but it was fairly obvious that he wasn't nearly as thrilled as his wife and children. While this kind of response is confusing at first, it makes sense when one understands how this man took the risk of moving his family thousands of miles to another country because he dreamed of a better life for them. Now that he was here, he realized that it was more difficult to get by in Canada than he had heard, and he felt a lot of guilt for dragging his family all this way only to experience greater poverty than they had left behind—at least for a time. Now he wasn't able to buy his children any Christmas presents or even provide enough for a special meal. He so desired for his wife and his children to look up to him, and he felt like such a failure for putting them through such difficulty. Then there was a knock at their door, and there were gifts and food, which was exciting for his family but in his mind only highlighted his own lack of provision. It was a well-intentioned gift that unintentionally treated the father of the home in an undignified way. Our gift, from the perspective of the husband, made him feel worse about himself. While this is a relatively mild mistake in comparison to the harm that can be caused, it does serve to help us think not only in terms of what our actions mean to us, but how they might be understood by those on the receiving end of our charity.

Sometimes our comments end up hurting people. Others have made such comments, and so have I. These are comments that may be well-intentioned but betray biases or are dismissive and belittling of the struggles someone is going through, or even demonstrate discriminatory attitudes. They may reveal that we care more about the fact that we helped than that the person we are supposedly serving is the one going through the crisis. We say things that can betray that we care more about patting ourselves on the back than we do about restoring dignity and a sense of hope to the people about whom we claim to care.

Bryant Myers writes candidly about his journey in learning to be more effective. "We had shared our successes and wept over our failures. . . . Thousands of hours of discussion, anguish, and discovery have taken place."[2] The experts have failed as well. Robert Lupton had a similar experience to the one that we did when arranging the delivery of Christmas gifts that left the father of the family feeling very undignified and discouraged. He writes, "Even the most kindhearted, rightly motivated giving—as innocent as giving Christmas toys to needy children—can exact an unintended toll on a parent's dignity. Inadvertently I had done just that. Not just this time but many times."[3] One of the first things we must realize is that no matter how much we try, we will never be perfect until we get to heaven, and there will be moments when we hurt others even though our goal and motive are to be a blessing. It has happened to experts, and it will happen to you if you begin to serve others. While this may seem discouraging, it is important to think soberly about such things if we have any hope of reducing the amount of harm we do and begin to actually be helpful in people's lives. Lupton writes, "While we cannot foresee all the potential consequences of our service, we should at least make some attempt to predict its impact."[4]

Something else that is incredibly important for us to learn is to properly evaluate situations before jumping in to help. While there are times of crisis when helping others needs to be done as quickly and efficiently as possible, other times it requires patience and thoughtfulness. Steve Corbett and Brian Fikkert write, "A helpful first step in thinking about working with the poor in any context is to discern whether the situation calls for relief, rehabilitation, or development. In fact, the failure to distinguish among these situations is one of the most common reasons that poverty-alleviation efforts often do harm."[5] To draw a comparison to the medical world, relief would be the equivalent of a paramedic, who comes during an emergency and provides temporary treatment, meeting the most immediate needs. In terms of helping others, this would be the workers that show up immediately after a natural disaster to help bring relief to those whose lives have been devastated by this disaster. This type of work is typically done *for* people, not always *with* people. While bedside manner is important for doctors as they go over potential treatment options with their patients, if a paramedic is treating an unconscious patient, the best option is for those with medical knowledge to act on behalf of those who have no ability in that moment to help themselves. Longer-term treatment and rehabilitation is the next stage, which in medical terms would be done by doctors who provide the care while in the hospital, helping their patient get well enough to get home, and the physiotherapists are the ones who help get patients ready to leave the hospital and who help after the patient leaves. Often there are various treatment options, and so the doctors, nurses, and therapists typically work together *with* their patient to decide which treatment options are preferable. In natural disaster situations, rehabilitation helps bring communities back to the place of being able to function in a relatively normal manner. This might involve helping rebuild roads or buildings, and is done together with the affected communities, but some things are still done for communities to help restore them. Development work, however, has a longer view in mind, and in the words of Corbett and Fikkert, "Development is not done *to* people or *for* people but *with* people."[6] To this end we again look at their general rule of thumb for avoiding harmful attitudes in our work: "Do not do things for people that they can do for themselves."[7]

As soon as one moves out of the *relief* stage, through *rehabilitation* and onward to *development*, the work being done begins to include primarily those who will benefit from the development. If we do not allow individuals and communities to take ownership for their own situations, we violate this principle and risk doing long-term damage. As Lupton says, "Giving that continues beyond the immediate crisis produces diminishing returns."[8] It doesn't take long to get to the development stage, either, and then working together becomes a necessity. When we look at the efficiency of modern industry and try to apply those same principles to long-term development work, meeting certain metrics might happen faster if these relationships are minimized in favor of prepackaged programs, but this so-called efficiency can end up doing great harm, and destroys what might have been gained otherwise. It undercuts free will and does not respect people's dignity. Doing things *for* people instead of *with* people fosters dependency, which leads to even greater helplessness instead of helping people help themselves.

Another way we can do significant damage pertains to our own attitude. When we approach people in poverty as if we have all the answers and are somehow superior, the implication is that those in poverty are inferior. When we do this, we end up reinforcing—if not outright creating—a sense of inferiority that writer Jayakumar Christian and others call the marred identity of the poor, which we talked about in chapters 5 and 7.[9] By approaching people with this type of god complex, we communicate to others that they are helpless and must rely on those who are supposedly superior. This does damage to both parties—the people serving and the people being served. When any of us stray from the truth of our identities, which are ultimately rooted in who God created us to be, we enter into a state of poverty. In these instances, we either underestimate our worth and so deface God's marvelous creation or we overestimate our worth and attempt to take the very place of God. Myers writes further, "No transformation can be sustainable unless this distorted, disempowering sense of identity is replaced by the truth. Healing the marred identity of the poor is the beginning of transformation."[10]

As long as humans are working with other humans, there is potential to do harm. As you will know by now, I too have made more than my fair share of mistakes. So we have several choices ahead of us: we can allow the possibility of failure to paralyze us into doing nothing, we can ignore these dangers and move forward ignorantly with the distinct possibility of doing more harm than good, or we can commit ourselves to learning and to doing what we can to prevent ourselves from doing excess harm as we seek to help. As you could probably guess, my hope is that you will embrace the third option; to quote Myers, "The poor deserved better than gifted amateurs with their hearts in the right place."[11] We can and we should do better. Rather than becoming discouraged because you have the potential to fail, be encouraged that you have the capacity to learn from your mistakes, or even better, to learn from the mistakes of others. In following Jesus and entering into the call of discipleship, we will inevitably be brought to places where we can and should make ourselves available to help others.

When we fail, as we inevitably will, then we must dust off the good old Christian teachings about confession, repentance, and perseverance. When we hurt someone, we apologize (confession), and then we make a change to prevent it from happening again (repentance). Then we continue on, despite our bruised egos, following Jesus as we take part in God's mission to the world (perseverance). While it might be easier to recruit volunteers by only talking about how amazing it is to serve God or how big of a difference one can make, I believe it is better to be truthful and honest about all of this, just as pastors and counselors are when couples prepare for marriage. When we seek to help others, we may end up hurting them. When we follow Jesus, things might get hard, we might be challenged, and we might follow Jesus imperfectly for a while. Yet follow Christ we must, as faithfully as we can.

FIFTEEN

Falling Forward

I AM A BIT OF A "DO IT YOURSELF-ER" kind of person. Well, "a bit" might be the understatement of the year. My wife chuckles when we walk through stores and something catches my eye, and I stop, stare for a bit while eying up this object, and quietly say, "Huh." She knows that this little sound means I just figured out how to build it myself. Having worked as a laborer in the home renovation and home building industry, I have gleaned a number of skills that have been helpful for the many little projects that I have taken on. The thing is, though, I don't know how to weld. There have been a bunch of times in my life where I have found myself in need of something to be welded, but I can't do it. In high school I took a class that taught us some very basic welding skills. When it came time to put these skills into practice, I was a dismal failure. I kept melting through the items I was trying to weld together, and eventually the teacher did my weld for me. I got the distinct impression that he thought I was hopeless when it came to this particular skill. After feeling like such a failure, I never tried welding again. Not trying again and learning this skill is something I regret, and it is a reminder for me that since I didn't put in the effort to learn from my mistakes, I am now completely unable to do this task. Thankfully, many in our congregation are or have been welders and fabricators by trade, so help abounds when I need it. Even still, I let my failure get the best of me, and instead of learning and growing through that experience, I simply gave up. In other areas of construction, I made many mistakes yet took a different posture: I learned how to fix the mistake and prevent it from happening again.

When I was a child, my father enrolled in an apprenticeship program to become a mechanic. When someone becomes an apprentice, they spend time studying and also spend time doing the work. My dad was in school for a couple of months out of the year, and the other ten months he would work as a mechanic under the supervision of a licensed and certified mechanic. While my dad knew a lot about cars going into this program, he still had much to learn, and had to approach his work with a sense of curiosity and a teachable spirit. That way, he could learn from the mechanic whom he was working under, as well as from the instructors in his classes. When he failed, those overseeing his work were able to tell him if the failure was a common but easily solved problem, or because of a faulty part, or caused by his own error, in which case he would be taught how to do better next time.

As we approach helping others and serving others as disciples of Jesus, I think we ought to embody the disposition of an apprentice. This really is what discipleship is supposed to be; however, something about the language of apprenticeship seems to give fresh meaning to the idea. As we live out our faith in this way, working to reduce the poverty in our communities and even around the world, I wonder what would happen if we would commit ourselves to learning more and to actively working at this alongside those who have more experience than we do. What if we were more open to correction and were willing to adjust the way we do things? What if we didn't approach this work believing we already know what to do but rather approached it believing that we truly need the help and wisdom of others for each situation we face? What if we allowed ourselves to be held accountable for the work we do? And what if we didn't give up at the first sign of failure or when things get complicated and messy? I suspect we would become much more effective in our efforts, as well as become better disciples of Jesus.

While discussion about how we can sometimes do harm when helping others might at first be discouraging, we should not allow our feelings of guilt or discouragement to prevent us from learning. In fact, we can learn from mistakes, both the mistakes we make and the mistakes of others who are brave enough to share with us. Robert Lupton says, "This national toxic-charity scandal can be reversed if we begin now to take preemptive action to change the compassion industry before it becomes discredited as a national embarrassment. I have seen that such change can happen."[1]

It is an exciting time in history to begin such a task, because of how this work has exploded in popularity in the past several generations, and the vast number of resources at our disposal that help us do this better. Individuals, NGOs, and even large-scale government projects have tried all manner of approaches, with some proving very effective and others failing miserably. There are experts who have devoted their lives to this work who can share from their experience and there are entire university programs dedicated to preparing frontline workers to serve in ways that help bring healing to various broken relationships instead of merely providing handouts that entrench dependence and rob people of their dignity. It is a privilege to exist at a point in history when these incredible resources can help us do better. Sadly, we are also at a point in time when there is still incredible need around us in our cities and small towns and around the world, and our service is needed just as much now as it has always been.

As I mentioned in the previous chapter, Robert Lupton, like myself, had an experience when Christmas gifts were brought to a needy family where the dignity of the father was harmed. Lupton shares in *Toxic Charity* about how his community learned from their failure and eventually changed the way they did things in order to better serve the community. He writes:

> The following Christmas we terminated our adopt-a-family gift-giving program. When well-resourced families called to contribute to a family, we asked if they would be willing to give an extra gift that year—the gift of dignity to the dads. Instead of delivering toys directly to the homes of the poor, donors were directed to bring unwrapped gifts to the Family Store where a large section was decorated as The Old Toy Shop. A bargain price was placed on each toy, and parents from the neighborhood were invited to come shopping for the special gifts sure to delight their children. Those who had no money were able to work at the store, earning what they needed for their purchases. In this way parents in the city experienced the same joy on Christmas morning as most other parents across the nation—seeing their children opening gifts they had purchased through the efforts of their own hands. That second Christmas our predictions proved spot-on: our low-income neighbors would much rather work to purchase gifts for their children than stand in free-toy lines with their "proof of poverty" identification.[2]

In this example, instead of items merely being donated, they are sold for reduced prices, allowing not only the children the joy of opening gifts, but parents the chance to take part in the joy of giving, and the gratitude of the children to be directed to their parents instead of some stranger. It is dignifying, uplifting, and unifying for the entire family rather than something that embarrasses the parents and causes them to feel that they are inadequate providers for their children.

Instead of just continuing to do things the way that they had before, Lupton's community decided to change how they did things, and the small shift in their methods ended up making a big difference to those they served. While offering food and gifts can be nice, offering it while also giving the gift of dignity is so much better.

When I was a child we would shop at what I remember calling "The Free Store." A group in the community used an empty storefront on Saturdays, and collected day-old goods and soon-to-expire items that grocery stores were about to throw out, and brought them to a place where people of the community could take them home for free. Being a child, I didn't understand the importance of dignity, and I was confused why my mother would act embarrassed every time we went in. I would, of course, ask for her to take home donuts, cookies, cakes, and individual little parfaits. Oh, how I coveted those little cups of dessert, but my mother almost always said no in the strictest of terms. This used to confuse me, because it was all free, so I knew we could afford it. One day, my mother explained to me that she didn't want to take anything from there that she wouldn't normally buy at the store, because she didn't want to be someone who took advantage of the generosity of others; but since we were in need, she got only the items that were necessary. She made one exception from time to time: she would let us pick out a package of bagels. I felt so wealthy on those days, being able to eat a bagel like the people on television. Since bagels are still technically bread and we could have them for breakfast, my mother allowed it, though I can't remember her ever buying bagels anywhere else. So while I felt rich on those occasions, because we could get a modest treat, my mother was always a bit sad and embarrassed. As I grew up I came to see that while we needed and appreciated the free groceries, every time she went to that "store," it was like wearing a giant sign that said, "Look at me, I'm poor!" which is not something anyone wants to feel. At the time I was too enthralled with my package of bagels to think much about my mother's responses to this outreach. Learning to change the way we do things in order to offer the gift of dignity when helping others is certainly one way that we can learn to "fall forward."

Yet this story from my upbringing also brings us to another side of this same coin. If someone in need feels uncomfortable receiving from others, one possible problem is that the charity is being done in a way that ignores dignity, but an equally possible problem is that the person on the receiving end of the gift struggles with the sin of pride. My mother is an amazing woman, but I suspect in this situation a good deal of her discomfort came from pride, rather than the disposition of those who ran this outreach. I shared a story in chapter 8 about how difficult it was for me to learn how to receive, and how it was the result of my own sinful pride lurking in my heart. Just because someone is in need does not mean that person is somehow exempt from the temptations we all face to allow our pride to get the better of us. While those on the giving end of a situation should examine their methods and attitudes to help bring dignity to a given situation, those on the receiving end must also make the choice to deal with their own pride as they receive from others. On the outside it may look the same from one situation to another, but in reality it may be that better methods are needed by the givers, or that a better attitude is needed from those receiving, or possibly both.

Furthermore, we shouldn't assume that poverty is a default position or something that we desire to be normal in anyone's life. We should always embrace a vision for the future that is hopeful for something better. This kind of hope should stem naturally from our gospel-centered hope that one day there will be no more suffering or crying or pain. The way of reducing poverty that brings the most dignity, whether at home or overseas, is a way that actually helps people to no longer be in poverty, which in turn enables them to offer a helping hand for others. In one sense, to even engage in poverty reduction work is to make a judgment call—not against an individual, but against the injustice of poverty. To desire to reduce poverty is to condemn poverty as something unwanted. In our work to bring dignity to people in the ways we serve them, we should not make the mistake of portraying poverty as the ideal way to live, just to make receiving help a bit more palatable in the face of someone's pride. Of course, we should treat people with dignity, but neither should we exempt them from realizing the dangers of pride, which can do as much damage to a person as being treated without dignity. I also want to note: the way we define poverty in material terms can make this complicated, because what one culture values might be drastically different from what other cultures value. I once heard a story about a missionary who thought that the jungle village where he served needed mattresses to sleep on, and arranged a huge charity event to make this happen, only to realize that the people in the village didn't like mattresses at all and preferred their traditional hammocks. What this illustrates is that while working to reduce poverty is to make a judgment call against such suffering, we must be careful not to label particular cultural preferences as an inferior way to live. Knowing the difference, however, can be challenging at times.

While I am skeptical of short lists of guiding principles because they often lack nuance, they can sometimes be a helpful *starting place* for discussion. *Toxic Charity* offers one such list, which contains some principles that give us food for thought in evaluating and reevaluating the way in which we engage in this important work. This list also has its limits, as we will discuss.

Never do for the poor what they have (or could have) the capacity to do for themselves.

Limit one-way giving to emergency situations.

Strive to empower the poor through employment, lending, and investing, using grants sparingly to reinforce achievements.

Subordinate self-interests to the needs of those being served.

Listen closely to those you seek to help, especially to what is not being said—unspoken feelings may contain essential clues to effective service.

Above all, do no harm.[3]

This list is succinct and offers some ideals for us to consider as we seek to minister to others. Sometimes, however, we can use lists like this to justify not doing anything, because we become too scared that we are going to fail, or because we can't check every box on the list when facing someone in need. So please do not allow a list like this to discourage you from using your gifts and resources to make a difference in the world. This list, however, might just make a great starting place for discussion with those in your community. What parts of it do you like? What parts do you find problematic? Is the list so narrow that nobody can realistically meet their requirements for being worthy of help? Or is it wise to be so discerning before helping at all? Better yet, take these questions and this list to those in your community who are already making a difference, and see what they have to teach you about it.

At times you might fail, and in those moments it would be wise to learn from your mistakes. Other times your efforts will fail through no fault of your own, and when that happens you should not give up either. There will be failures on your part, and likewise there will be failures on the part of those you seek to serve. Sometimes you will hinder matters, and sometimes other people will be the hindrance. Sometimes our programs can do better to bring dignity into the equation, and sometimes those we serve must wrestle through their own pride in order to realize there is no shame in receiving help from others. Sometimes the problem is that we are shaming others, other times the problem is that they are shaming themselves. Sometimes our actions may set up dependency that can become a prison, and other times the prison exists primarily in the heart and mind of the individual we are serving. These are all possibilities, and sometimes they may all be going on at the same time.

If we can avoid becoming paralyzed by our mistakes, we stand to learn a lot that will enable us to do better and serve others more carefully in the future. It will result in healthier relationships and more effective ministry. It will safeguard people's dignity and avoid dependency. Though you may fail, allow the feelings of humiliation to become humility, and allow the guilt to lead you to confession and repentance. Allow your ignorance to give way to insight, and let your mistakes guide you to healthier ministry. Learn to fall forward. In the words of Pope Francis, "The church must step outside herself. To go where? To the outskirts of existence, whatever they may be, but she must step out. Jesus tells us, 'Go into all the world! Preach! Bear witness to the Gospel!' (see Mark 16:15). But what happens if we step outside ourselves? The same as can happen to anyone who comes out of the house and onto the street: an accident. But I tell you, I far prefer a Church that has had a few accidents to a Church that has fallen sick from being closed. Go out, go out!"[4]

SIXTEEN

When Small Acts Grow Big

IT WAS JUST ANOTHER DAY FOR HIM, or at least it started out that way. He was living on the streets, struggling with a devastating addiction. This day, however, would end up being a turning point in his life that would lead to him conquering his addiction, finding work and housing, and eventually moving into a role in church ministry. He had no idea how much his life was about to change. He had been on the street for years, and as usual he was feeling broken and worthless to the world. I wonder how many people passed him by that day, like other days, while averting their gaze—pretending they were suddenly distracted by something else. I wonder how many times someone made a rude comment to him or glanced at him with disgust written all over their face. I wonder how many people looked at him with pity; not sympathy or kindness or compassion, but simple, condescending pity. The day went on, and that night he was hanging out at a bus terminal. He approached a middle-aged woman to simply ask for the time. She looked at him as if he was just another human being, not someone substandard or defective, but like a fellow person and literally just gave him the time of day. He knew it was profound in that instant, but I'm sure he couldn't imagine how important this moment would become in his life. Someone looked at him like a person, not like an object of pity or scorn. Someone treated him with a small amount of dignity, which caused him to wonder if there was something of worth left in him. This moment turned into a cascading series of choices and circumstances that would bring healing to this broken man. This simple, small act ended up becoming the catalyst for the transformation of a person who was a homeless addict into a person who has been made whole and now is actively helping others. As Greg deGroot-Maggetti from Mennonite Central Committee shared this story with me,[1] I sat in wonder at the power of how small acts of love can sometimes break down the walls that hold people captive.

Writer Kayla Robbins discusses how devastating it can be for people struggling with homelessness when they are continually ignored instead of simply having their existence acknowledged. She observes, "After a while, homeless people who are subjected to this treatment begin to feel as if they were ghosts watching the world but not able to fully participate in it. If they try to strike up conversations, their words fall on deaf ears. They're ignored, dehumanized, and invisible."[2] While we may ignore many people as we walk down the street, people living on the street are constantly ignored, and so simply acknowledging them in a small and dignified way can make a difference. It shouldn't be the only thing we ever do to help, but it is something that costs us nothing and can have a profound impact on others. Doing this can also help change the way we look at people experiencing poverty— and in at least one case it led to miraculous transformation.

There are so many times when small acts of love end up being seeds that are planted that grow into something large that bears great amounts of fruit in someone's life. In one of the rooms at The Simple Way in Philadelphia, a little board on the shelf says "Small things, great love" and contains doodles of what appear to be dandelions, that invasive weed so many of us are trying to get rid of. And this is exactly how Shane Claiborne talks about the spread of the kingdom of God: like a weed that spreads one seed at a time and can eventually overtake lawns, fields, towns, and cities. This is consistent with how many scholars talk about Jesus' parable about the mustard seed and the parable of the leaven in the dough. These two are sometimes called twin parables, as they appear directly beside each other in Matthew (13:31-33) and Luke (13:18-21), and both parables reinforce one another. In the parable of the mustard seed, Jesus talks about how an incredibly small seed can grow into a large plant, and in the parable of the leaven, he teaches about how the leaven is almost invisible, yet it spreads through the entire dough and is what makes the bread rise. Both of these parables communicate an incredible truth about following after Jesus: what we perceive as little things often end up becoming something large in God's kingdom.

Linda Chamagne, the founder of The Bridge urban ministry in the city of Saskatoon, told a story about a woman who came into their ministry center.[3] This woman had come there several times before, but it had been a long time since Linda had seen her. As the woman walked in, Linda excitedly welcomed her by name, and the woman began to cry. Linda was confused, thinking there must be some kind of tragedy going on, and in a sense there was. This woman was feeling broken and in that moment was deeply and profoundly moved on an emotional level simply because Linda remembered her name. A small thing ended up having a tremendous impact on someone that day. While it is a tragedy that so few remembered her name, Linda's small act of love was powerful in that moment.

My dad came from a very difficult upbringing, and he often credits one family in particular for helping make his life better, a couple I came to call Uncle Danny and Aunt Judy. My dad talks about Danny as a kind of father figure who helped him to learn more about parenting, being a better husband, man, and so on. What this couple did was not something most of us would call very profound. They would come visit and drink coffee, or we would share a meal together. In short, they just spent time with us. For someone with a background like my father's, this made a big difference in his life at the time. Danny and Judy lived out the gospel around the dinner table and in our living room, showing God's love in small and tangible ways, most often just through time spent together as friends. When we talk about God's love in large and cosmic ways, like the rising sun or the delicate balance of the earth, it can be difficult to process or understand. Yet when the love of God is translated into a cup of coffee, or incarnated in a lovingly made home-cooked meal, small acts somehow translate the glory and love of the divine into something that we can actually begin to digest. Even though Danny and Judy didn't and weren't able to eliminate the financial poverty in our lives, they helped make life more joyful and meaningful, and in doing so did more for our family than the free food programs that helped fill our bellies.

In his book *Nonviolent Action*, Ron Sider tells the account of Leymah Gbowee, a peace activist from Liberia.[4] Gbowee was a single mother who had witnessed a great deal of violence in her country. There had been years of civil war, and she and the entire country had been devastated by the violence. One day she had a dream, and in this dream someone called out to her, telling her, "Gather the women and pray for peace!" She thought that there must have been some mistake, that God must have gotten the wrong person. In the end she did gather women to pray for peace. This simple act of corporately gathering to pray for peace became a catalyst for a national movement. Prayer led to peace marches, which led to an opportunity to sit down with the dictator to ask for peace, which in turn led to him being willing to negotiate with the opposing leaders in the country. When the mediations almost soured, the women of Liberia surrounded the building, insisting they not abandon these deliberations but continue on until they could come to terms for peace. Even while Gbowee felt unworthy to gather the women to pray, this small act of inviting others to join her in petitioning God to bring peace ended up toppling a dictator and ending years of civil war, all without firing a single bullet. Gbowee was awarded the Nobel Peace Prize for her incredible work.

Tom Davis, author of *Red Letters* and *Fields of the Fatherless*, shares a story of his own upbringing. His mother left his stepfather, and in this time of life they began attending a church. Tom spoke with the church's youth pastor, Kurt, sharing some of their tragic story. Kurt invited him to spend some time with his family. Davis writes, "On that special Saturday, Kurt treated me like his own child. He took me on a picnic, bought me ice cream, and played soccer with me. They were simple acts of kindness, but they made a profound impact on me. Kurt had absolutely nothing to gain personally. He just poured out biblical, selfless love to a little boy who desperately needed it. I had never felt such genuine love from anyone in my entire life. That experience changed me!"[5]

Time after time, the small acts of ordinary people have been used by God to do amazing things. Consider another story from the New Testament in John 6:1-13. Thousands of people gathered around Jesus. They were curious about this person who had been doing miracles and teaching in their area, so they came to see for themselves. Jesus observed that the people were hungry, and asked the disciples to feed them; his disciple Philip estimated that the cost to feed everyone was more than half a year's wages. Well, Jesus asked, what *was* available? One boy offered to share his lunch: five loaves of bread and two fish. I would have loved to see the look on the boy's face at what happened next. Jesus instructed everyone to sit down, and started to share this boy's lunch with others. Miraculously, they didn't run out of food, and thousands of people were fed. Furthermore, they required twelve baskets just to contain all the leftovers. God has a special ability to take what little we offer and multiply it in whatever way the Lord sees fit.

Every small act of love contains within it the potential to brighten someone's day or even change someone's life. Every little offering we give can be used by God for something great, and every time we take part in God's mission we become a part of God's ever-unfolding story. Don't underestimate the power of being faithful in the small things.

SEVENTEEN

When Small Acts Stay Small

"I DON'T LIKE YOUR QUESTION and I'm gonna push back a bit at this." I can't remember the first time I heard an answer like this in the middle of an interview, but such responses no longer caused me any panic. After about six years of experience in radio doing countless interviews, I came to learn that these were the moments to listen. In the early days I would have gotten flustered and possibly even defensive, but over time I came to learn that when people answer in this way, they are revealing a danger or an ignorance somewhere in my question that needs to be addressed. This particular time, I was in the office of professor Ray Vander Zaag at Canadian Mennonite University. I had just asked him about stories of people who do small things that yield big results. After this initial response to my question, he told me that he really struggled with it for a few reasons. Professor Vander Zaag began to explain that emphasizing the way small things can have a big impact can create unhealthy expectations and toxic attitudes, though he definitely believes in the importance of people being consistent in living out small acts of kindness and love.

If we only see fit to engage in small acts of service that have a big impact, then we may never get started, because we will always be waiting for the right moment. It can become a kind of obsession with grandeur, all the while not being willing to do our part unless a disproportionate impact can act as another proverbial feather in our hat. A big problem with this kind of attitude is plain and simple pride. We are no longer doing those little things to serve others simply because it is the right thing to do or out of the goodness of our heart, but rather because we want to have some story to tout about a time we changed someone's life. To make matters even worse, if we have such a self-centered approach to Christian service, then we may end up only doing things that are self-serving. The more we go down this road, the more we will be tempted to neglect the small acts of love that we ought to be doing, because we only want to do things that are flashy or things that feed our own ego. Our acts of service become too calculated. We become like politicians so accustomed to the halls of power that the only time they serve others or care for needy children is when the cameras are rolling. When we only engage in small acts of love because we want big results, we must be careful to check our motives and expectations.

Now, small actions can have a large impact, but we must also learn to be okay if our small daily acts of faithfulness in following Jesus produce only a small result. We also may never even see the full impact of our service, and I believe that is okay too. In the words of Vander Zaag, "If doing this depends on seeing big change and being in control of the results then it's easy to get discouraged. Here the Anabaptist perspective of presence— doing the small thing—is really important. What I actually do is more important than the results of what I do. If our doing it depends on knowing that we are going to create a big result, then again we are playing God and we are trying to control things too much ourselves, and it doesn't stay part of our obedience and responsiveness; instead of allowing God to work through us, we try to become gods ourselves."[1] While we can rejoice in the moments when small acts of love have a big impact, we must learn to do these things simply because God wants us to do them, regardless of how large or small of an impact we have.

This, of course, is different from doing things ignorantly. This kind of logic is sometimes misapplied to situations where our charity is damaging, yielding little positive result and plenty of negative outcomes. We may convince ourselves that the best course of action is to simply keep doing what we are doing, thinking that being faithful to a particular way of doing things is synonymous with being faithful to God. The reality is, however, that the damage we do may in fact be because of our own failure to serve others in a way that respects the dignity of others or makes wise use of resources.

I once met a man who often talked about "the bigger picture." I was so impressed with his charisma, vision, and excitement, so I got involved in what he was doing. As time went by, however, I came to see that his "bigger picture" didn't include the way he treated people in his everyday life, and included plenty of shortcuts that helped him accomplish his particular vision— while leaving a trail of hurting people in his wake. While I am most definitely an advocate of taking a step back and examining the big picture to see the way our actions can play out and to be more effective in what we do, sometimes I also think we need to have a smaller picture. If our heads and hearts are proverbially stuck in the clouds, then we might not be able to see the toes we step on or the dignity we crush because we are too focused on our "big picture." This is the beautiful example we see in the Bible: a God who fills the entire universe, yet who came down to our level, coming as a vulnerable baby, born to a family in poverty. As Jesus made his way in this world, he cared for the oppressed and downtrodden. Jesus, God in the flesh, who brought galaxies into existence merely by saying the word, was concerned about those whom the rest of his creation seemed to reject. If there ever was someone who had a big-picture view of things, it would be God. Yet we see that Jesus didn't let this stop him from caring for the people others ignored. If we can't serve others in small, everyday, ordinary ways, then I wonder if the "big picture" we are obsessed with is really the same as the one at which God is looking.

* * *

Sometimes the work we do won't miraculously turn into something huge in someone's life. In fact, most of the time it won't. That doesn't mean that we should stop. So long as we are actually helping in a way that isn't toxic or damaging, we should keep on serving others in small, everyday ways. Simply doing what is right and good, even if others don't view us as a hero, is still the right thing to do. In fact, it's probably even more so, because when we try to become someone's savior, we are attempting to take the place of God in their life.

In the apostle Paul's first letter to the Corinthians, he writes about using the gifts that God has given them. He discusses how some people can be jealous of others or look down on others because of the different roles they play in God's kingdom. He uses the analogy of anatomy, and how different parts in one body play different roles while being part of one body. Then he makes a fascinating statement. He says, "Those parts of the body that seem to be weaker are indispensable, and the parts that we think are less honorable we treat with special honor. And the parts that are unpresentable are treated with special modesty, while our presentable parts need no special treatment. But God has put the body together" (1 Corinthians 12:22-24). When we think about serving others, we might not always aim to be someone who simply and consistently does those small things for God's kingdom. Yet as Paul points out, just because we may play a role that isn't flashy or popular doesn't mean that we are less important. Just because we may only be able to do small things for God's kingdom doesn't mean that we shouldn't do them or that they are less important. Sometimes our small roles will stay small, but that doesn't make them any less vital.

I should also mention that there are times when God calls some people to extravagant acts of kindness or generosity. Throughout the pages of Scripture and throughout the history of the church, there have been moments where God invites people to give more extravagantly than the average person would be capable of giving. Or there are people God asks to do things that require a lot more concentrated effort, like moving overseas to work with a nonprofit or spearheading a large fundraiser for a specific cause. It may be that God is giving you a vision for something so big that it takes courage to even admit that this dream exists. If this resonates with you, I encourage you to explore what you might be called to do.

Regardless of whether you feel led to serve God in ways that are extravagant or ordinary, our faithfulness to God is at its finest when the gospel is lived out in tangible ways in our relationships with our neighbors, families, and communities. Filling stadiums of people to cheer for the person at the podium isn't going to make the big difference. What we need is more people willing to love others like Jesus loved them—in our living rooms and around our tables, on our street corners and in our businesses, and yes, even in our churches. I believe that in order for the kingdom of God to grow, our view of the gospel must, in a sense, become smaller, though not any less powerful. The apostle Paul says that "God chose the foolish things of the world to shame the wise; God chose the weak things of the world to shame the strong" (1 Corinthians 1:27). I believe we need more people who are willing to be fools for God, rejecting the building of our own empires in favor of investing in God's kingdom by loving those made in God's image. We need people to see those around them as God sees them, not as their credit rating talks about them. We need to become a people that stops believing that "bigger is better," and to start believing, really believing, that better is better. Once we get over our obsessions with grandeur, we can begin to see that healing is often slow, messy, and not nearly as flashy as we have been led to believe.

We need to recapture a view of greatness that is more consistent with the teachings of Jesus. When his disciples were arguing about who would be the greatest in God's kingdom, Jesus responded to their selfish bickering by placing a child in front of them and saying, "Whoever takes the lowly position of this child is the greatest in the kingdom of heaven. And whoever welcomes one such child in my name welcomes me" (Matthew 18:4-5). We must recapture a view of greatness that has less to do with fame and spectacle and more to do with sincere and unpretentious acts of love. When we learn to be content to serve without fame or fortune, we begin the journey to serving in ways that more closely align with the ways of Jesus.

CONCLUSION

Faithful in Small Things

I WAS ALMOST THIRTY YEARS OLD by the time I could grow a mustache. I had tried periodically for more than fifteen years, but it was always patchy and sparse. It took so long, in fact, that by the time I was able to grow one it had some grey hairs in it. In the years before I could grow a mustache successfully, I would, of course, be teased for my poor excuse for facial hair. Eventually I began to respond by telling people, "Hey, this is a biblical principle right here!" They would be confused but intrigued, and would chuckle and then ask how I came to that conclusion. Well, I referenced the parable of the three servants in Matthew 25:14-30, and told them about the faithful servant of whom the master said, "You have been faithful with a few things; I will put you in charge of many things" (Matthew 25:23). My meager mustache was me being faithful in trying to grow the few hairs that I had, and I was hoping and trusting that in time God would give me more to care for. Eventually the good

Lord did in fact bless me with the ability to grow a mustache—even though I am still waiting for the gift of a full beard.

In the parable of the three servants from Matthew, each servant is given a different amount of money by their master. Some are given more and some less. The master intends that they invest the money he has given them and put it to work, in order to yield some kind of return on his investment. The first two servants put this investment to work, and their work is rewarded. One makes great profit, the other little, but the master is pleased with each of these servants and gives them more of which to be in charge. The last servant does nothing with this money and simply returns it to the master without making use of this opportunity. The master is furious with this servant, as he didn't do anything. Sometimes people who feel that they have little to offer don't give anything because they feel that their contribution is just a drop in an ocean and isn't worth anything. I know I have felt that way. Yet this is the kind of mindset we must avoid. Regardless of how much or little we have to offer, we must be faithful in doing what we can. We are not responsible for fixing everything or everyone. We are not the saviors of the world, but we as Christians do represent the Savior and can point people to the God who both made and saved the world.

With the vast amount of need in each of our communities and the daunting amount of suffering around the world, we can become paralyzed by the amount of poverty we may see. We might not know where to start, and we may constantly feel that what we are doing isn't enough. The truth is, we cannot do it all, we cannot be everywhere, and none of us have enough resources to fix everyone's problems. However, you have been placed in a particular community in a particular time in history with particular relationships to particular people. You have a specific personality and unique gifts, which can be utilized to help someone. You also have places in your life where you experience brokenness, and where you are vulnerable, which may find healing as you follow Jesus, or which may even help bring healing to others as you seek to serve.

Or perhaps you can't even think of anyone you know personally whom you would consider to be living in poverty. Well, there could be a couple of reasons for that. The first is that you may live in a neighborhood or community that is overwhelmingly affluent, in which case I would like to invite you to consider whether you can make a change in your life so that you can intentionally come into contact with people from different parts of society.

Another reason you may not know others who live in poverty is perhaps because you proverbially and literally haven't opened your eyes to it. If you see poverty as simply homelessness, and don't know how to see it as something more, then there could be people without enough to eat or with tremendous difficulties whose need you don't see but who are living right next door or down the street. If this resonates with you, then perhaps try extending your circle of friends and getting to know people better in a way that makes it safe for them to share with you the struggles that they might face.

Wherever you find yourself, I simply want to encourage you to follow in the footsteps of Jesus. In chapter 2 we talked about the example of Jesus, and about how all our efforts to make a difference in the world ultimately come back to following the example and teachings of our Savior and the example of God throughout the pages of the Bible. Do what you can to be the hands and feet of Jesus, wherever you are or wherever God calls you to go. And remember, you don't have to and shouldn't do this alone. In the words of Henri Nouwen,

I have found over and over again how hard it is to be truly faithful to Jesus when I am alone. I need my brothers or sisters to pray with me, to speak with me about the spiritual task at hand, and to challenge me to stay pure in mind, heart, and body. But far more importantly, it is Jesus who heals, not I; Jesus who speaks words of truth, not I; Jesus who is Lord, not I. This is very clearly made visible when we proclaim the redeeming power of God together. Indeed, whenever we minister together, it is easier for people to recognize that we do not come in our own name, but in the name of the Lord Jesus who sent us."[1]

One of the best ways to get started is to volunteer with an organization that has a proven track record of effectively and holistically helping others in ways that honor their dignity, and to spend time learning from them. Get involved together with other believers, be willing to learn, and do whatever it is that God has enabled you to do. Also remember that there is tremendous poverty around the world, and while our gifts of time and energy will primarily be used in our own communities, remember that our financial generosity can make a huge difference around the world even though we may not be able to see the results with our own eyes. One preacher put it this way, "Money is a miraculous thing. It is your personal energy reduced to portable form and endowed with power you do not possess. It can go where you cannot go; speak languages you cannot speak; lift burdens you cannot touch with your fingers; save lives with which you cannot deal directly."[2] We can both serve in the communities where God has placed us and generously give to trustworthy organizations in order to help people in other corners of the world where poverty is much greater.

Sometimes when people try to encourage other believers to care for those living in poverty, they get accused of peddling a false gospel, other than the gospel we read about in the Bible. That is something that I do not wish to do. I want to point people back to the good old gospel message that our spiritual ancestors have followed for two thousand years. In the early church, the apostle Paul spent time with the apostles James, Peter, and John. They discussed theology at length, and eventually these leaders gave their approval to Paul and his teachings. Then, as Paul concludes his recollection of this meeting, he says, "All they asked was that we should continue to remember the poor, the very thing I had been eager to do all along" (Galatians 2:9-10). This is what the gospel inspires us to do. It isn't some new or trendy fad or some weird modern take on the teachings of Scripture. The gospel of Jesus Christ is what motivates and inspires all the work that we are talking about in our discussion. This book is not an attempt to change the gospel or to neglect the importance of the other teachings of the Bible. Rather, my hope is that it will similarly encourage you in the way that the apostles encouraged Paul: as we follow Jesus may we remember those in poverty and do what we can to help in ways that honor our Lord by showing love to all those made in God's image. May we give generously, love lavishly, and serve humbly. May we seek dignity for our neighbors and build relationships of mutuality. May we seek to bring healing to the broken relationships that result in poverty. May we seek to dismantle systemic injustice, and in its place build systems that protect the vulnerable and embrace equality—because if we are to truly follow Jesus, what other path is there?

A Note to Rural Readers

WHILE THERE ARE TIMES when rural areas are obviously full of poverty, in some small towns it can sometimes be incredibly hard to see. Many times, people who are homeless will make their way to cities because of a greater concentration of services like soup kitchens, shelters, and food banks. While it may be harder to spot at times, poverty is often just as present in smaller communities. When engaging in a discussion about poverty, I was once told that it wasn't relevant for people in a particular rural community. According to the person I was talking to, "We don't have any poverty here." While this comment might seem to be encouraging because of how nice this community must appear, I was deeply saddened by it because I had done some work in this community and was well aware of poverty that was still ravaging many families and individuals. Not to mention that this perspective on poverty views it as only a lack of money, which also neglects the various kinds of broken relationships that need healing. It wasn't that poverty didn't exist in this community, it just wasn't as visible. In order for this poverty to be made visible, one must have some kind of relationship with those experiencing poverty. These relationships need to have enough mutual trust that those in need are willing to open up about their struggles, as experiencing financial poverty can be embarrassing and can be steeped in a sense of shame. In order to help, one must know that a need exists, and seeing the needs can be a bit more difficult when the number of people sleeping on rural park benches isn't as high as in urban areas.

One of the challenges for small churches in general is a lack of resources to establish consistent programs. There often isn't money to hire staff to oversee a wide variety of social programs, or the number of people in the church is simply too small to run them entirely on volunteer power. There have been many small church pastors who look at their big-city megachurch counterparts with envy, wishing they could offer big, expensive, and flashy programs. Yet small churches offer a unique benefit that can be of tremendous value to a community: they can be flexible and often respond quickly to individual situations. When emergencies happen, if a large church doesn't have a program in place, it can be hard to receive help because it is primarily managed through programs with boards, committees, budgets, and a specific mandate. When a need falls outside the purview of the project or program, it is easy for it to fall through the cracks and be left uncared for. In small churches, however, when an emergency situation doesn't require a large program but rather needs a response that is tailor-fit for a particular circumstance, a small church is usually much more able to help. Fewer decisions have to go through church budgets and board approval, and more can be done simply by rallying people together for a common cause in a moment of crisis. Smaller churches are often more relational in nature, which can also be incredibly beneficial for addressing the broken relationships that result in poverty. In this way, small churches in rural communities can still be powerful catalysts for helping people in times of need, even if they don't have big programs or huge budgets.

Another significant way that rural churches can help address and reduce poverty is by working together with the various organizations in the community that may be needed in times of crisis. In the county where we live, a collaborative program was started that brought together various sectors in order to respond to individual needs and provide specialized care for specific situations—preferably before there is a full-blown crisis. This program includes representatives from healthcare, child welfare, legal aid, law enforcement, food banks, shelters, and other community-minded organizations, bringing in the relevant parties to help families and individuals in need. All that a family needs to do is consent to meeting with this group, and pastors or other representatives can refer them for such a meeting. All the relevant organizations will help address the various needs in whatever ways they can. They have found that it cuts through the red tape and simplifies matters, making access to services easier, and giving frontline workers options for how to holistically help people they encounter. Furthermore, such an approach means those in need of help don't have to go to every organization and explain their dire circumstances every time, which can be traumatic and humiliating. Instead, it is done once with all the relevant organizations present, and then all of them can begin to act in ways that help bring resolution to the issues people are facing. While this isn't exactly a big program, it helps the smaller organizations work together for the betterment of those in their communities and enables more holistic and flexible care for those in poverty. This kind of teamwork can go a long way in rural communities.

Another significant need for those in rural communities is transportation. People often have to commute to other communities for work, which requires being able to get there. In these circumstances, helping people purchase a reliable vehicle is something that can enable them to become self-sufficient because it means they can get themselves to places of employment. One local car dealership in my county refurbishes older cars, then gives them away to people who need them. A ministry called God's Garage in Texas does something similar, giving away vehicles to women in need, including single mothers, widows, and wives of deployed military personnel. Most of us will have heard the saying "Give someone a fish and they eat for a day, but teach them to fish and they can eat for a lifetime." Giving the gift of transportation is the modern equivalent of giving someone a fishing rod. It is the tool that enables them to work and provide for themselves. Cities usually have public transportation systems, but rural communities often lack such services, thus considering a ministry that helps provide transportation is an incredibly practical way to serve your community. Furthermore, providing transportation for people who are housebound can also be a way to help. Older folks who are unable to drive, or those with medical conditions preventing them from having a driver's license, must rely on others to get them to their medical appointments or even to go grocery shopping. In rural communities this can be a huge issue once again because of a lack of public transportation.

I have noticed a peculiar phenomenon that happens when resources are limited: creativity often increases. Instead of just being able to pay for a certain program or service, people have to get creative to accomplish a particular goal. In our congregation, we went through a financial crisis when we couldn't even budget a few hundred dollars for a benevolence fund because the church budget was so low. We refused to believe that money is the be-all and end-all of ministry, so we brainstormed other ways of helping. Instead of our customary gift of a grocery store gift card to people in need, we involved our entire congregation and did food drives when we encountered someone in need. We kept the names anonymous to protect recipients' dignity, and the one who had a relationship with that person would deliver the groceries, together with someone else from church to foster a sense of teamwork and accountability. When we switched to this model, we found that our congregation began to open their eyes a bit more to see the needs around them, because they now had a way to help those in their sphere of influence. Instead of just ignoring needs because they didn't know what to do, it gave an avenue for people to show love to their neighbors, friends, and family. While it wasn't a perfect solution, it has blessed many people and has been a way to serve God in our community by showing love to others. In the first year alone, we gave away more than we had in the past several years combined, even while having a significantly lower budget as a church. Sometimes in the pressure of scarcity, the good Lord helps us be more creative as we seek to be faithful to Jesus.

I am saddened by how often rural ministry can be disparaged by some, when the people in our small towns and rural areas are loved by God just as passionately as those in urban centers. The reality is that rural churches also have many in their midst who are experiencing poverty, and often suffer from a lack of financial stability themselves as a church. As such, I want to remind you that those of us in rural contexts can still make a difference in reducing poverty, even while we may lack financial resources. While this theme is repeated throughout this book, I repeat it again: just because you may be a small church in a small town doesn't mean your ministry to your community is any less sacred or less vital to the mission of God. Continue to do what you can, and find creative ways to serve others and so bring glory to our God—and no matter how forgotten your community may feel, God is with you in this sacred and holy work.

Further Reading

10 – A Guide for Cities Reducing Poverty by Brock Carlton and Paul Born. Tamarack Institute, 2016.

The Church of Mercy: A Vision for the Church by Pope Francis. Loyola Press, 2014.

Crazy Love: Overwhelmed by a Relentless God by Francis Chan. David C Cook, 2008.

Dignity: Seeking Respect in Back Row America by Chris Arnade. Sentinel, 2019.

God's Country: Faith, Hope, and the Future of the Rural Church by Brad Roth. Herald Press, 2017.

The Irresistible Revolution: Living as an Ordinary Radical by Shane Claiborne. Zondervan, 2006.

Making Neighborhoods Whole: A Handbook for Christian Community Development by Wayne Gordon and John M. Perkins. InterVarsity Press, 2013.

Red Letters: Living a Faith That Bleeds by Tom Davis. David C Cook, 2010.

Rich Christians in an Age of Hunger: Moving from Affluence to Generosity by Ronald J. Sider. Thomas Nelson, 2015.

Toxic Charity: How the Church Hurts Those They Help and How to Reverse It by Robert D. Lupton. Harper One, 2011.

The Upside-Down Kingdom, 25th anniv. ed., by Donald B. Kraybill. Herald Press, 2018.

Walking with the Poor: Principles and Practices of Transformational Development, rev. ed., by Bryant L. Myers. Orbis Books, 2011. First published 1999.

When Helping Hurts: How to Alleviate Poverty without Hurting the Poor . . . and Yourself by Steve Corbett and Brian Fikkert. Moody Publishers, 2012. First published 2009.

Acknowledgments

IN THE WILD JOURNEY OF LIFE, and the series of events that led me to write this book, I would be remiss not to first of all acknowledge God's work in my life. The Lord has been my strength and my rock, and the only reason I have anything of value to offer. I also want to thank my wife, Emily, who has not only put up with my constant working, wondering, and writing, but also spurred me on and encouraged me time and again. I am thankful for our children, Jasmine, Marshall, and Finnley, who model childlike faith and who inspire me constantly with their tender compassion and acts of love for others.

I want to thank the staff at Herald Press for all their work, especially my editor, Dayna Olson-Getty. Thank you for partnering with me on this project, and for doing all your amazing work during the COVID-19 pandemic no less. I am grateful for the friends, family, and colleagues who served as beta readers for the first rough draft of this book: Mark Dalley, Erin Vermont, Russell Doerksen, and Layton Friesen. Thank you for offering your wisdom to this work, and for shaping my perspective through the years gone by.

I am grateful for my congregation at New Life Christian Fellowship for the way they seek to follow Jesus, and for graciously allowing me to take a sabbatical to write. I am thankful for the way my parents offered such hospitality to so many others, and despite the challenges of our life, I will always be grateful for the many lessons I was able to learn. I also want to thank Joe and Mary Elias for their example to me of living out the gospel in so many ordinary ways that have had such a profound effect on me and so many others. I also want to thank my friend and colleague Terry Smith for how he encouraged me to do more writing, and for helping me hone those skills over the years.

Lastly, I want to thank you, dear reader, for taking an interest in how to better serve our world. We need more people who are willing to be faithful in small things—I truly believe that this is how we will change the world!

Notes

Part 1: The Bible on Poverty
1   Steve Corbett and Brian Fikkert, *When Helping Hurts: How to Alleviate Poverty without Hurting the Poor . . . and Yourself* (Chicago: Moody, 2012), 53.

Chapter 1
1   Bryant L. Myers, *Walking with the Poor: Principles and Practices of Transformational Development* (Maryknoll, NY: Orbis Books, 1999), 27.
2   Michael J. Ruszala, *Saint Mother Teresa of Calcutta: A Witness to Love* (Boston: Wyatt North, 2015), 76.
3   Beth Guckenberger, *Reckless Faith: Let Go and Be Led* (Grand Rapids: Zondervan, 2008), 101.
4   Jody Porter, "Children of the Poisoned River," *CBC News*, 2017, https://www.cbc.ca/news2/interactives/children-of-the-poisoned-river-mercury-poisoning-grassy-narrows-first-nation/.
5   Porter.

Chapter 2
1   Shane Claiborne, "Session 1: Our Homeless Leader," interview by Kevin Wiebe, *Pov.ology*, November 16, 2016, https://www.youtube.com/watch?v=ESUxwDSxtZQ.
2   Steve Bell, "Session 1: Our Homeless Leader," interview by Kevin Wiebe, *Pov.ology*, November 16, 2016, https://www.youtube.com/watch?v=ESUxwDSxtZQ.
3   Joseph L. Mangina, *Karl Barth: Theologian of Christian Witness* (Louisville: Westminster John Knox, 2004), 145.
4   Claiborne, "Session 1: Our Homeless Leader," *Pov.ology*.
5   Stuart Murray, *The Naked Anabaptist* (Harrisonburg: Herald Press, 2010), 51–70.

6   Shane Claiborne, "Session 2: Putting Your Money Where Your Mouth Is," interview by Kevin Wiebe, *Pov.ology*, November 16, 2016, https://www.youtube.com/watch?v=s5CI3DV6SyE.

7   General William Booth, cited in Geoff Ryan, *10 On the Army: Re-imagining the Salvation Army for the 21st Century* (Canada: Rubicorn Books, 2007), 117.

8   Donald B. Kraybill, *The Upside-Down Kingdom*, 25th anniv. ed. (Harrisonburg: Herald Press, 2018).

Chapter 3

1   Søren Kierkegaard, *Provocations: Spiritual Writings of Kierkegaard*, ed. Charles E. Moor (Farmington, PA: Plough, 2002), 201.

2   Gary A. Haugen, *Just Courage: God's Great Expedition for the Restless Christian* (Downers Grove, IL: InterVarsity Press, 2008), 76.

3   Bruxy Cavey, "Session 2: Putting Your Money Where Your Mouth Is," interview by Kevin Wiebe, *Pov.ology*, November 16, 2016, https://www.youtube.com/watch?v=s5CI3DV6SyE.

4   Leon Morris, *The Gospel according to Matthew*, The Pillar New Testament Commentary (Grand Rapids: W. B. Eerdmans; Leicester, UK: Inter-Varsity Press, 1992), 634.

5   Claiborne, "Session 2: Putting Your Money," *Pov.ology*.

6   Mark Galli, "The Unfortunate Pedigree of the Missional Church," *Christianity Today*, June 5, 2019, https://www.christianitytoday.com/ct/2019/june-web-only/unfortunate-pedigree-of-missional-church.html.

7   C. S. Lewis, *The Great Divorce* (San Francisco: HarperCollins, 1973), 73–74.

8   Bryant L. Myers, *Walking with the Poor: Principles and Practices of Transformational Development*, rev. ed. (Maryknoll, NY: Orbis Books, 2011), 4.

9   Stanley Hauerwas, *A Community of Character: Toward a Constructive Christian Social Ethic* (Notre Dame, IN: University of Notre Dame Press, 1981), introduction, Kindle.

10   Greg Pearson, "Session 2: Putting Your Money," *Pov.ology*.

Chapter 4

1   Gary V. Smith, *Hosea, Amos, Micah*, The NIV Application Commentary (Grand Rapids: Zondervan, 2001), 554.

2   Henri J. M. Nouwen, *The Wounded Healer: Ministry in Contemporary Society* (New York: Image Doubleday, 1972), 78–79.

Chapter 5

1   Anne McIlroy, "Drunk in Charge," *The Guardian*, December 28, 2001, https://www.theguardian.com/world/2001/dec/28/worlddispatch.annemcilroy.

2   "Ralph Klein Changed My Life, Says Former Homeless Man," *CBC News*, March 31, 2013, https://www.cbc.ca/news/canada/calgary/ralph-klein-changed-my-life-says-former-homeless-man-1.1329520.

3.   Names have been changed to protect privacy.

4   Steve Corbett and Brian Fikkert, "Corbett, Fikkert: Knowing the Difference Key to Helping the Poor," *Times Free Press*, November 8, 2009, https://www.timesfreepress.com/news/opinion/columns/story/2009/nov/08/1108-knowing-the-difference-key-to-helping-the/241577/.

5   People like my friend Kyle Mason and others within the many Indigenous communities have done excellent work in helping educate others around the unique issues that Indigenous Canadians face. Learning about this is a bit of a tricky thing for those of us who are non-Indigenous, because while it is our own responsibility to educate ourselves, we also should not speak in the place of those whom we should be learning from. Thankfully, many Indigenous people have been and are willing to share and teach. My view is that while we need to take responsibility for our own education, we must also view as a precious gift the stories and education that are shared by Indigenous community members. We cannot demand that they teach us, but neither can we properly learn without them, so our approach must avoid tokenism and be marked by humility, appreciation, and sincerity.

Chapter 6

1   Ronald J. Sider, "Session 5: What about the Gospel?," interview by Kevin Wiebe, *Pov.ology*, November 16, 2016, https://www.youtube.com/watch?v=9X53IpEZRHQ.

2   Shannon Doerksen, "Am I My Body? The Importance of Materiality," *Small but Brave: Reflections on Theology, Infertility, and Life in General* (blog), October 4, 2014, https://smallbutbrave.wordpress.com/2014/10/04/am-i-my-body-the-importance-of-materiality/.

3   Donald B. Kraybill, *The Upside-Down Kingdom*, 25th anniv. ed. (Harrisonburg, VA: Herald Press, 2018), 99.

4   Henri J. M. Nouwen, *In the Name of Jesus: Reflections on Christian Leadership* (New York: Crossroad Publishing, 1989), 76.

5   Nouwen, 79.

6   Pope Francis, *The Church of Mercy: A Vision for the Church* (Chicago: Loyola Press, 2014), 100–101.

7   Pope Francis, 17.

8   Patrick Franklin, "Bonhoeffer's Missional Ecclesiology," *McMaster Journal of Theology and Ministry* 9 (2007–8): 124–25, https://www.mcmaster.ca/mjtm/pdfs/vol9/articles/MJTM_9.6_FranklinBonhoeffer.pdf.

9   Sider, "Session 5: What about the Gospel?," *Pov.ology*.

10 Sider.

11 Quoted in William Barclay, *The Gospel of Luke* (Louisville: Westminster John Knox, 2001), 138.

12 General William Booth, *In Darkest England: And the Way Out* (New York: Funk & Wagnalls, 1890), 45.

13 Kyle Mason, "Session 5: What about the Gospel?," *Pov.ology*.

Chapter 7

1 Damian Zane, "Barbie Challenges the 'White Saviour Complex,'" BBC, May 1, 2016, https://www.bbc.com/news/world-africa-36132482.

2 Teju Cole, "The White-Savior Industrial Complex," *The Atlantic*, March 21, 2012, https://www.theatlantic.com/international/archive/2012/03/the-white-savior-industrial-complex/254843/.

3 Barbie Savior, "While the man who holds my heart is across the ocean, I still must carry on my important work," Instagram photo, February 14, 2017, https://www.instagram.com/p/BQgJ2GOlwSL/.

4 "Who We Are," No White Saviors, accessed June 27, 2019, https://nowhitesaviors.org/who-we-are/.

5 Ray Vander Zaag, "Session 3: Responding to Poverty," interview by Kevin Wiebe, *Pov.ology*, November 16, 2016, https://www.youtube.com/watch?v=ikOVIJai-R8.

6 Bryant L. Myers, *Walking with the Poor: Principles and Practices of Transformational Development*, rev. ed. (Maryknoll, NY: Orbis Books, 2011), 145–46.

7 Vander Zaag, "Session 3: Responding to Poverty," *Pov.ology*.

8 Henri J. M. Nouwen, *In the Name of Jesus: Reflections on Christian Leadership* (New York: The Crossroad Publishing Company, 1989), 17.

9 Nouwen, 17.

Chapter 8

1 Steve Corbett and Brian Fikkert, *When Helping Hurts: How to Alleviate Poverty without Hurting the Poor . . . and Yourself* (Chicago: Moody Publishers, 2012), 109, Kindle.

2 Patrick Franklin, "Bonhoeffer's Missional Ecclesiology," *McMaster Journal of Theology and Ministry* 9 (2007–2008): 124, https://www.mcmaster.ca/mjtm/pdfs/vol9/articles/MJTM_9.6_FranklinBonhoeffer.pdf.

3 Franklin, 124.

4 Franklin, 124–25.

5 A toonie is a Canadian two-dollar coin, which in Canada is about enough money to buy a cup of coffee.

6 Ray Vander Zaag, interview by Kevin Wiebe, November 26, 2015, Winnipeg.

Chapter 9

1 Bruce K. Alexander, "Addiction: The View from Rat Park," *Bruce K. Alexander* (blog), 2010, https://www.brucekalexander.com/articles-speeches/rat-park/148-addiction-the-view-from-rat-park.

2 Johann Hari, "Everything You Think You Know about Addiction Is Wrong," filmed June 2015 in London, UK, TED Global video, 14:34, https://www.ted.com/talks/johann_hari_everything_you_think_you_know_about_addiction_is_wrong.

3 Hari.

4 Chris Arnade, *Dignity: Seeking Respect in Back Row America* (New York: Penguin, 2019), 282.

5 Jonathan Hollingsworth and Amy Hollingsworth, *Runaway Radical: A Young Man's Reckless Journey to Save the World* (Nashville: Thomas Nelson, 2015), 203.

Chapter 10

1 Greg deGroot-Maggetti, "Session 1: Our Homeless Leader," interview by Kevin Wiebe, *Pov.ology*, November 16, 2016, https://www.youtube.com/watch?v=ESUxwDSxtZQ.

2 Mother Teresa, *A Simple Path* (New York: Ballantine Books, 1995), 79.

3 Geoffrey Nelson, Leslea Peirson, and Isaac Prilleltensky, eds., *Promoting Family Wellness and Preventing Child Maltreatment: Fundamentals for Thinking and Action* (Toronto: University of Toronto Press, 2001), 51.

4 Nelson, Peirson, and Prilleltensky, 117.

5 Nelson, Peirson, and Prilleltensky, 108.

6 Nelson, Peirson, and Prilleltensky, 108–9.

7 Brooke C. Feeney and Nancy L. Collins, "A New Look at Social Support: A Theoretical Perspective on Thriving through Relationships," *Personality and Social Psychology Review* 19, no. 2 (May 2015): 113–47.

8 Douglas LaBier, "Why Positive Relationships Are Needed for Emotional Health," *Psychology Today*, September 26, 2014, https://www.psychologytoday.com/us/blog/the-new-resilience/201409/why-positive-relationships-are-needed-emotional-health.

9 Cindy Pom, "UK Launches New Campaign to Tackle Loneliness," *Global News*, June 17, 2019, https://globalnews.ca/video/5401407/uk-launches-new-campaign-to-tackle-loneliness.

10 Henri J. M. Nouwen, *In the Name of Jesus: Reflections on Christian Leadership* (New York: The Crossroad Publishing Company, 1989), 61.

11 Nouwen, 61–62.

Chapter 11

1 Ronald J. Sider, *Rich Christians in an Age of Hunger* (New York: W Publishing, 1997), 21.

2   Sider, 23.

3   It should also be mentioned that in many nations, if one would live as many are forced to in the Global South, social services would define it as neglect and children would be placed in foster care. Furthermore, in places like Northern Canada where I grew up, it would be extremely difficult to survive through the harsh winter, so basic survival requires a more substantial dwelling. Factors like this contribute to the higher cost of living and the necessity of having higher incomes than in many places in the world. I am convinced that it is improper to evoke guilt over these realities, as I also believe it is the God-given responsibility of parents to provide for and care for their children.

4   Kevin Wiebe, "Stewardship and Simple Living," in *Holy Wanderings: A Guide to Deeper Discipleship* (Steinbach/Winnipeg, MB: Christian Mennonite Conference, Evangelical Mennonite Mission Conference, and Evangelical Mennonite Conference, 2019), 53–60.

5   Henri J. M. Nouwen, *In the Name of Jesus: Reflections on Christian Leadership* (New York: Crossroad Publishing Company, 1989), 35.

Chapter 12

1   Ronald J. Sider, "Session 4: Do No Harm," interview by Kevin Wiebe, *Pov.ology*, November 16, 2016, https://www.youtube.com/watch?v=f6AaEMwBsuM.

2   Bryant L. Myers, *Walking with the Poor: Principles and Practices of Transformational Development* (Maryknoll, NY: Orbis Books, 1999), 27.

3   Wayne Gordon and John M. Perkins, *Making Neighborhoods Whole: A Handbook for Christian Community Development* (Downers Grove, IL: InterVarsity Press, 2013), 62, Kindle.

4   Shane Claiborne, "Session 3: Responding to Poverty," interview by Kevin Wiebe, *Pov.ology*, November 16, 2016, https://www.youtube.com/watch?v=ikOVIJai-R8.

5   Shane Claiborne, "Session 6: The Power of Small Things," interview by Kevin Wiebe, *Pov.ology*, November 16, 2016, https://www.youtube.com/watch?v=F2UbLzeSP8I.

6   Martin Luther King Jr., "A Time to Break Silence" (sermon, Riverside Church, New York City, April 4, 1967), available at http://www.americanrhetoric.com/speeches/mlkatimetobreaksilence.htm.

Chapter 13

1   Greg Pearson, "Session 3: Responding to Poverty," interview by Kevin Wiebe, *Pov.ology*, November 16, 2016, https://www.youtube.com/watch?v=ikOVIJai-R8.

2   Robert D. Lupton, *Toxic Charity: How the Church Hurts Those They Help and How to Reverse It* (New York: HarperOne, 2011), 191, Kindle.
3   Steve Corbett and Brian Fikkert, *When Helping Hurts: How to Alleviate Poverty without Hurting the Poor . . . and Yourself* (Chicago: Moody Publishers, 2012), 164, Kindle.
4   Corbett and Fikkert, 164.

Chapter 14
1   Robert D. Lupton, *Toxic Charity: How the Church Hurts Those They Help and How to Reverse It* (New York: HarperOne, 2011), 4–5, Kindle.
2   Bryant L. Myers, *Walking with the Poor: Principles and Practices of Transformational Development*, rev. ed. (Maryknoll, NY: Orbis Books, 2011), 2.
3   Lupton, *Toxic Charity*, 33.
4   Lupton, 132.
5   Steve Corbett and Brian Fikkert, *When Helping Hurts: How to Alleviate Poverty without Hurting the Poor . . . and Yourself* (Chicago: Moody Publishers, 2012), 99, Kindle.
6   Corbett and Fikkert, 100.
7   Corbett and Fikkert, 109.
8   Lupton, *Toxic Charity*, 129.
9   Christian Jayakumar, *God of the Empty-Handed: Poverty, Power and the Kingdom of God* (Brunswick East: Acorn Press, 2011).
10   Myers, *Walking with the Poor*, 178.
11   Myers, 2.

Chapter 15
1   Robert D. Lupton, *Toxic Charity: How the Church Hurts Those They Help and How to Reverse It* (New York: HarperOne, 2011), 7–8, Kindle.
2   Lupton, 38–39.
3   Lupton, 8–10.
4   Pope Francis, *The Church of Mercy: A Vision for the Church* (Chicago: Loyola Press, 2014), 99.

Chapter 16
1   Greg deGroot-Maggetti, "Session 6: The Power of Small Things," interview by Kevin Wiebe, *Pov.ology*, November 16, 2016, https://www.youtube.com/watch?v=F2UbLzeSP8I.
2   Kayla Robbins, "Making Eye Contact with Homeless People Is Important," Invisible People, May 22, 2019, https://invisiblepeople.tv/making-eye-contact-with-homeless-people-is-important/.

3   Linda Chamagne, "Session 6: The Power of Small Things," *Pov.ology*.

4   Ronald J. Sider, *Nonviolent Action: What Christian Ethics Demands but Most Christians Have Never Really Tried* (Grand Rapids: Brazos Press, 2015), 103–19.

5   Tom Davis, *Fields of the Fatherless: Discover the Joy of Compassionate Living* (Colorado Springs: David C Cook, 2008), 59–60.

Chapter 17

1   Ray Vander Zaag, "Session 6: The Power of Small Things," interview by Kevin Wiebe, *Pov.ology*, November 16, 2016, https://www.youtube .com/watch?v=F2UbLzeSP8I.

Conclusion

1   Henri J. M. Nouwen, *In the Name of Jesus: Reflections on Christian Leadership* (New York: Crossroad Publishing Company, 1989), 58–59.

2   Harry Emerson Fosdick (1878–1969), quoted in Edwin Friesen, *God, Money, and Me: Exploring the Spiritual Significance of Money in Our Lives* (Winnipeg, MB: Mennonite Foundation of Canada, 2004), 2.

The Author

KEVIN WIEBE is an Anabaptist writer, pastor, and the creator of *Pov.ology*, a small-group curriculum on poverty and the church that has been used around the world and featured in publications across the United States and Canada. Wiebe grew up among the working poor, with parents who had a standing family rule that "there is always room for one more," even as they struggled to get by themselves. He is senior pastor of New Life Christian Fellowship in Stevenson, Ontario, a rural congregation whose members are primarily Mennonite immigrants from Mexico. He has degrees from Providence University College and Conrad Grebel University College and is an ordained minister in the Evangelical Mennonite Conference. He and his wife, Emily, have three children.